CANOEING MANITOBA RIVERS

John Buchanan

VOL. 1 SOUTH

Rocky
Mountain Books

Front cover: Barry Catt and Carol Kristjansson at Split Rock on the Bloodvein. Photo: Clyde Cowan.

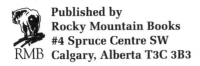

**Published by
Rocky Mountain Books
#4 Spruce Centre SW
Calgary, Alberta T3C 3B3**

The publisher gratefully acknowledges the assistance provided by the Alberta Foundation for the Arts and by the federal Department of Canadian Heritage.

COMMITTED TO THE DEVELOPMENT OF CULTURE AND THE ARTS

Canadian Cataloguing in Publication Data

Buchanan, John, 1938-
Canoeing Manitoba rivers

Contents: Vol. 1, South.
ISBN 0-921102-55-0(v.1)

1. Canoes and canoeing--Manitoba--Guidebooks. 2. Rivers--Manitoba--Guidebooks. 3. Manitoba--Guidebooks. I. Title.
GV776.15.M3B82 1977   797.1'22'097127   C97-910165-4

Contents

Acknowledgements

When I started writing this book I believed that writing was a solitary craft. I discovered that while the actual writing can be solitary, researching the information is anything but. I would like to thank all the people whose contributions made this book possible: The librarians at the Winnipeg Public Library and the University of Manitoba taught me how to use microfilm readers and how to use the library, and didn't realize they were contributing to a manuscript; Terry, Sue-Ann and Mariette showed me how to find maps and air photos at the Surveys and Mapping library and let me use the facilities freely; Rick Wilson of Natural Resources, Parks Branch, Heather Geddes of Global Village and Colette Fontaine of Manitoba Tourism lent material support.

A special thanks goes to Gerry and Maureen Reckseidler, Marcel Richot and Jeannine Macaulay who were always willing to drop everything and go canoeing for a day or a week. But most of all thanks to Chris for her support and encouragement of all my crazy ideas.

Disclaimer

There are inherent risks in canoeing wilderness rivers. Although the author has alerted readers to locations where particular caution is to be exercised, flooding and changes in water levels can alter a river dramatically. Paddlers are expected to adequately assess their skills and the threat from natural hazards.

Canoeists use this book entirely at their own risk, and the author disclaims any liability for any injuries or other damage that may be sustained by anyone paddling any of the routes described in this book. The decision to paddle a river or run a rapid lies solely with the individual.

Biography

John "Bucky" Buchanan is an avid canoeist who resides in Winnipeg, but calls the rivers of Manitoba his home from April to October. He enjoys all aspects of canoeing, but has a preference for wilderness tripping. He recently published a series of "RiverRunner Guides" to Manitoba that are available from the Surveys and Mapping Branch, 1007 Century Ave., Winnipeg.

Introduction

With long summer days, cool evenings and an abundance of sunshine, Manitoba offers ideal summer canoeing opportunities. Whether you are looking for a quiet day paddle, an extended wilderness trip, a challenging rapid or a lake to explore there is a trip for you in Manitoba.

This book is a sampling of canoe trips in the southern half of the province. Volume II will cover the northern half. Use the guidelines to select a trip suitable for your ability and leisure time.

Canoeing in Manitoba has in some ways changed little since the days of the voyageurs. The equipment has become much lighter and more durable. Large-scale topographical maps are available for all the rivers. But information on class of rapids, length of portages and availability of campsites is still passed on verbally.

When I started canoeing, I didn't know many other canoeists; this lack of information combined with inexperience lead to several near disasters. With more experience I started travelling farther afield, and I found that reliable information was still difficult to acquire. Mapmaker Real Berard has produced a series of large-scale maps that are fascinating from an historical viewpoint but not useful for navigation.

Being a compulsive notetaker, I soon compiled a set of notes on the rivers I had paddled. Over time this led to becoming a source of information to the paddling community in Winnipeg, but on a causal basis. I decided that this information should be made available to a wider audience and in a more formalized manner, hence the justification for this book. To complete the book, I repaddled all the rivers mentioned plus a few that I hadn't explored.

No doubt many interesting canoe routes have been missed. Suggestions or comments on other routes or extensions and variations of routes covered are most welcome. Please address these to the author, care of the publisher or the Manitoba Recreational Canoe Association.

Explore Manitoba by canoe as a solitary pursuit, with a close friend, with your family or through the activities of clubs and organizations across the province. Enjoy recreational canoeing or pursue competitive events. Involvement also encompasses social events, evening meetings and programs, clinics and coaching.

Canoeing in Manitoba is easy. You will need a canoe, paddles and a lifejacket. For your first forays these items can be rented. Topographical maps of your planned route should be carried. If you are camping overnight a tent, sleeping bag, cook stove and utensils are necessary. Sunblock and bug repellent are recommended. Canoeists wear a wide variety of clothing. One acquaintance wears rubber boots while another carries only sandals. So wear whatever is comfortable and ignore the experts. Refer to the camping and medical checklist for suggestions on appropriate gear, but use your own judgement on what to take.

So get your canoe, grab a paddle and a partner, and discover the waterways of Manitoba. With 100,000 lakes and countless rivers, streams and creeks there is a route suitable for everyone. Don't rush your trip. The phrase "the joy is in the journey" refers to canoeing. Descriptions and maps guide you along the trip but be aware that changes in water levels can alter a river dramatically. A placid meandering stream in a dry year can become a raging torrent in a wet year. Even a heavy rainfall can change the character of a small river.

Welcome to Manitoba

Manitoba lies at the heart of Canada, sprawling over 650,000 sq km. Within these boundaries a wide diversity of landscapes and ecosystems is found. The variety and beauty of Manitoba are among its assets as a province for canoeing, cycling, skiing, hiking or backpacking.

Most of Manitoba's one million residents are clustered in the southern third of the province, concentrated around the Red River. Winnipeg is the largest city, with 60 per cent of the provincial population. Other major centres include Selkirk, Portage la Prairie, Brandon, Dauphin, The Pas, Flin Flon and Thompson. The continuing migration to urban centres and mechanization of farming means that the river valleys are reverting to nature. It is unusual to see anyone other than other canoeists on the southern rivers and you will usually have the river to yourself in the non-agricultural portion of the province.

Getting to Manitoba

Situated in the centre of Canada, Manitoba is accessible by road (especially by the Trans-Canada Highway running east to west across the province), by plane from neighbouring provinces and states, by train and by bus. American citizens require proof of citizenship to cross the border into Manitoba.

Landforms

In order to know what type of canoeing to expect it is necessary to understand a little of the geography of Manitoba. Manitoba can be divided into four physiographic regions:

Located in the far north is the Hudson Bay Lowland. This is an undulating plain of low elevation overlain with marine clays. Ancient beach ridges are the main relief features. The rivers are large, high volume rivers such as Churchill, Nelson, Seal and Hayes and are braided with many shallow channels. It is hard to follow the main channel and there is often poor camping.

The Precambrian Shield is the largest physiographic region, slashing across the province from northwest to southeast. It is a fairly level though uneven, rocky terrain. The glaciers so deranged the drainage that what is left is a maze of swamps, beaver ponds, lakes, streams, and some great rivers like the Bloodvein and Pigeon. There are many waterfalls where rivers cross granite ridges.

The Manitoba Lowlands are responsible for Manitoba's flat reputation. The bottom of glacial Lake Agassiz is the lowest and flattest part of Manitoba. Over one-sixth of the province consists of fresh water, including the three large lakes plunked in the centre of these lowlands, Lakes Winnipeg, Winnipegois and Manitoba. Here we find typical prairie rivers, slow moving and meandering like the Red and Assiniboine. Sand deposits from the glacial period provide some topographic relief in the Manitoba Lowlands, especially east of the Red River in a region now cloaked by provincial forests, and farther west in the extensive sand dunes of the Carberry region.

The rise of the Manitoba Escarpment, slicing northwest through the province, announces the Manitoba Uplands. It is characterized by broad river valleys, formed by large glacial rivers and runs between mountainous uplands such as Porcupine, Duck, Riding and Turtle mountains. The rivers are typically small, low volume streams such as the Souris, Shell and Valley canoeable only during spring. There is some exceptionally good canoeing where the rivers cross the escarpment or flow off the mountain.

Vegetation and Wildlife

Manitoba vegetation reflects the general physiographic regions, as well as local influences such as climate, soil and topography. The northern tundra, the boreal forests of the Shield, and the parkland and prairie of the south characterize the vegetation along Manitoba rivers.

Canoeing on Manitoba rivers brings you in close contact with wildlife. The many Wildlife Management Areas are home to white-tailed deer, coyotes and porcupines. Beavers can be found in all of the rivers. Manitoba is internationally known for its variety of birds—the best place to observe them is the river corridors, especially during spring migration.

Climate

Manitoba's continental climate is characterized by long, hot, dry summers ideal for canoeing. Average monthly weather data for Winnipeg summers is:

	May	June	July	Aug.	Sept.
Avg. Max. temp. (C)	18.0	23.1	25.9	24.7	18.4
Avg. Min. temp.	4.5	10.5	13.3	11.8	6.3
Mean Daily temp.	11.3	16.8	19.6	18.3	12.4
Highest temp.	37.0	36.7	37.8	40.6	36.2
Lowest temp.	-11.1	-3.3	11	0.6	-7.2
Days with rain	10	11	11	11	11
Avg. Rainfall (mm)	65.7	80.1	75.9	75.2	53.3
Thunderstorms	2	6	8	7	3

Average temperatures for Winnipeg are slightly higher than the rest of the province. Southwestern Manitoba receives less precipitation on fewer days while east of Lake Manitoba is a little wetter and the north somewhat cooler. The averages can be deceiving, as Manitoba's climate is characterized by its variability, although extended periods of dry and wet spells are common, often lasting for weeks. Starting a trip with good weather usually means that weather will be pleasant for the whole voyage. The trick is predicting when the good weather will arrive.

Population

The province is proud of its broad ethnic background, and includes people of native, French, Scottish, English, Métis, Ukrainian and Mennonite origins. These peoples, plus Chinese, Lebanese and many others, have retained their food preferences, which are catered to by supermarkets. This wide availability of food choices makes preparing tasty, easily transported meals effortless.

Getting Involved

Recreational canoeing is a mainstay of the Manitoba Naturalist Society outdoor program. The group offers evening outings, day trips and weekend excursions. The Manitoba Recreational Canoe Association offers instruction and some trips.

Canoeing and camping have been incorporated into the programs of various other broadly mandated groups. For example, the Boy Scouts and Girl Guides' organizations offer day trips and overnight excursions. The YMCA and YWCA include canoeing and tripping in the camp program, culminating in a six week-long canoe trip for older children.

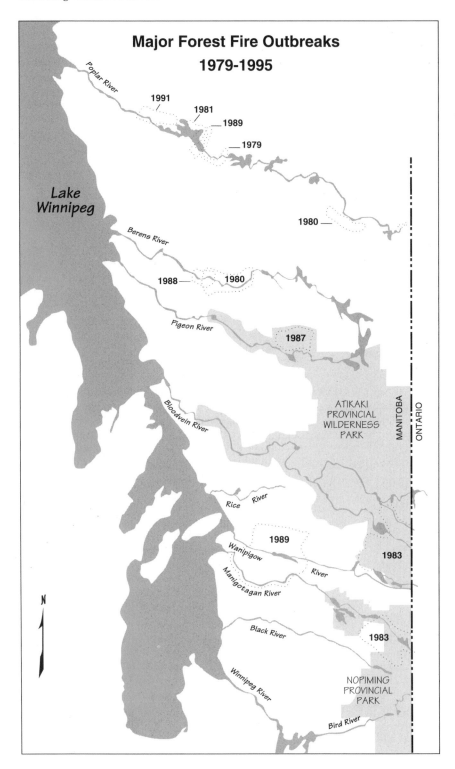

Major Forest Fire Outbreaks
1979-1995

Getting Further Information

Maps

The maps provided in this book show general views of the routes. Once you have decided on a particular route pick up the detailed topographical maps recommended, as greater map detail is needed than can be provided here.

The Surveys and Mapping Branch carries topographical maps showing contours, geographical details, and some rapids and waterfalls, but not all. Check the contour lines where they cross the river—this usually indicates a rapid. Air photos can be used to check fine details such as the exact location of a portage. The Surveys and Mapping Branch also has a series of maps prepared by Real Berard covering many of the routes mentioned in this book. These maps are an excellent source of historical and cultural information, but are too large a scale to be used for navigation. Bucky's RiverRunner Guides are also available from Surveys and Mapping. These guides are intended to supplement topographical maps by rating the rapids and locating the portages. Printed on kelvar, they can be carried on canoe trips.

Manitoba Parks Branch prepares maps of most parks in the province. These can be used as a supplement to topographical maps. Designated campsites are marked and other useful information is shown such as lodges, boat launches and portages.

Tourist Information

Travel Manitoba is the provincial government department responsible for tourist information. The Manitoba Explorers Guide lists parks, historic sites and general information about the province. The Manitoba Events Guide gives detailed listings of special events and festivals throughout the province, while the Travel Value Guide offers savings on accommodations, dining and attractions. The most detailed accommodation information is found in the Manitoba Accommodation and Campground Guide, which lists campgrounds, hotels, bed and breakfasts, and farm vacations. Manitoba Fishing and Hunting Adventures has a detailed list of outfitters and air charter services. Obtain these publications and others from Travel Manitoba.

Background on the Province

Canoeists looking for historical and cultural information on Manitoba will find several overview histories, plus many books on the history of specific localities within the province. Check local bookstores, many of which have a Manitoba or western Canada section, or try the Legislative Library or the public library. For history, browse through *Manitoba, the Province and the People* by K. Coates and F. McGuinness (Hurtig Publishers, Edmonton, 1987). A recent introduction to the literature of the province is *Section Lines: A Manitoba Anthology* (M. Duncan, ed., Turnstone Press, Winnipeg, 1988).

The best background information for canoeists interested in expanding their natural history and ecological understanding is found in *Natural Heritage of Manitoba: Legacy of the Ice Age* (J. T. Teller, ed., Manitoba Museum of Man and Nature, Winnipeg, 1984). A variety of geographical, biological, economic and social information is mapped in the *Atlas of Manitoba* (T. Weir, ed., Manitoba Department of Natural Resources, Winnipeg, 1983). Another excellent book on the geography of Manitoba is *The Geography of Manitoba: its Land and its People* (J. E. Welsted, J. C. Everitt, C. Stadel, ed., University of Manitoba Press, 1996). Look for guides to prairie wild flowers and Manitoba birds, butterflies, mammals and plants published by the Manitoba Naturalist Society or the Department of Natural Resources.

Access

The logging roads shown on this map can be used to access rivers for shorter trips. They are built and maintained by the Pine Falls Paper Co. but are open to the public. Travel with caution and watch for logging trucks, as they are not expecting recreational traffic. These roads are not suitable for typical cars as they are rough and very soft in the spring.

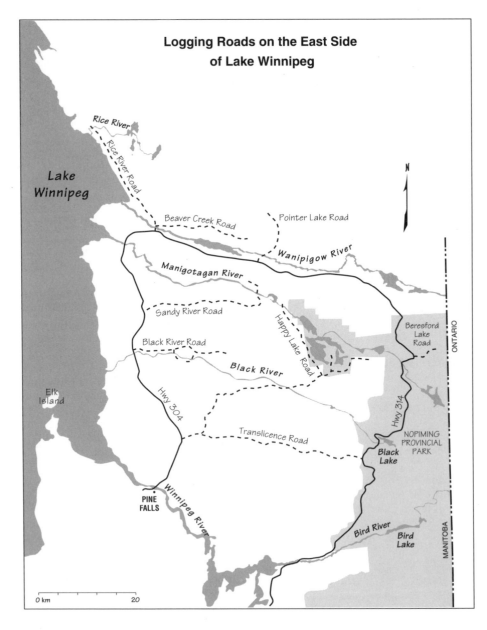

Canoe Trip Checklist

Here is a checklist of some of the more important items to take on a canoe trip. It is by no means an all-inclusive list. Use it as a basis to start your own personal list.

Personal Items
lifejacket
insect repellent, sunblock, lip balm
whistle
personal medications
toilet paper and lighter, soap, towel, toothbrush, toothpaste, floss
bowl, spoon, knife, water bottle, water purifier
sleeping bag, sleeping pad
fleece, rain pants and jacket, short and long sleeve shirts, wind pants, wind jacket, hat, canoe shoes, camp shoes, bug jacket, toque, long underwear, paddling gloves
ear plugs for charter plane

Group Items
canoe, paddles, bailer, sponge, bow and stern ropes, throw bag
tent, ground sheet, rain-fly, poles, stakes, tarpaulin
maps, map case, compass
stove, fuel, grill
pots, fry pan, spatula, wooden spoon, cutting board, water bag, folding saw
waterproof backpack
garbage bags, rubber bands, twist ties
first aid kit
scouring pad, net bag, wash basin

Repair Kit
duct tape
stove repair kit
sleeping pad sealer
needle and heavy thread
canoe patch kit

Bear Protection
Absent from this list is any form of bear protection. Only once have I ever seen a bear in the wild and it was on the far side of a lake. Likewise very few of my acquaintances have ever been bothered by bears, but it does happen. In Manitoba, the only bears you will encounter are black bears, and all they want is your food. Following the usual precautions of hanging food and not eating in tents should eliminate most danger. Of all the deterrents, "bear bangers" (a pencil gun with a flare) make the most sense. They work at a reasonable distance, unlike sprays, and don't require a direct hit like shotguns. However, they won't stop a determined bear. Still, I question if I could find and correctly use one of the stronger deterrents in an emergency. For a complete discussion of this topic read *Bear Attacks: Their Causes and Avoidance* by S. Herrero, Nick Lyons Books, Winchester Press, 1985.

First-Aid Supplies

In order to have safe and enjoyable outings a first-aid kit is essential. The contents of the kit will depend on the length and difficulty of the trip and the distance from medical help. In my experience the most common injuries are burns from fires and minor cuts and bruises. More important than the first-aid supplies is having the knowledge and skill to use the contents properly. Personally, I always have a nurse, doctor or wilderness medical technician as my paddling partner on extended trips!

4" by 4" sterile dressings to apply pressure to a wound
non-adherent dressings such as Telfa or Spenco Second Skin
wound closure strips to bind together deeper cuts
knuckle and regular adhesive strips
elastic bandage
surgical tape
bandage scissors
triangular bandage
safety pins
10cc irrigation syringe for cleaning wounds
latex surgical gloves for your protection
tweezers
antiseptic towelettes
moleskin or Comspeed for blisters
sam splint; a lightweight universal splint that can be fashioned as a cervical collar, arm, leg or ankle splint
CPR Microshield for mouth-to-mouth resuscitation
Betadine solution or iodine tablets
Polysporin antibiotic ointment
glucose paste and hypothermia thermometer for hypothermia
ibuprofen such as Advil for relief of inflammation and pain
aspirin or Tylenol
antacid tablets
aloe vera gel for burn relief
cortisone cream for muscle soreness
antihistamine like Benadryl
antiseptic solution such as Tincture of benzoin
cotton-tipped applicators
antifungal cream like Tinactin
temporary dental filling like Cavit
scalpel
fire starter
waterproof matches
candle
space blanket

Although it may seem cheaper to buy all these components and assemble your own first-aid kit, you'll save both time and money by purchasing a kit designed specifically for paddlers. The following companies make them and can direct you to a dealer:

Adventure Medical Kits, (800) 324-3517
Outdoor Research, (206) 467-8197
Atwater Carey Ltd., (303) 444-9326
Chinook Medical Gear, Inc., (800) 766-1365

How to Use This Book

The canoe trips described in this book are arranged alphabetically by river. To select a route, flip through the descriptions or refer to the summary maps and tables. The maps show the location of all routes described. Select a route based on geographical location or difficulty. All of the routes can be shortened by changing the starting or finishing point. Difficult sections can be avoided or included by choosing an alternate access point. The alternate access points are noted in the river descriptions.

The route descriptions all have a similar structure. The main title gives the river name. A sketch map is provided and its scale is dependent on the distance covered. For each route, several titled paragraphs provide explicit information on:

Type A general description of the route and the surrounding terrain.

Difficulty The rating is based on the Canadian Recreational Canoe Association (CRCA) classification system for canoeists in open canoes and on moving water.
- A Beginner can effectively use all the basic strokes from the bow and stern and can negotiate Grade I rapids with assurance.
- An Intermediate paddler can line the canoe around rapids; can ferry, set and carry out eddy turns; can give assistance to swamped paddlers and can negotiate Grade II rapids.
- An Advanced paddler can negotiate fast, turbulent water; is skillful in the bow and stern in Grade III rapids and can sometimes successfully run Grade IV rapids.

International River Rating System
- Class I: Small and regular waves; passages clear; occasional obstructions
- Class II: Passages clear and wide with occasional boulders or small ledges
- Class III: Waves numerous, high, irregular with rocks and narrow passages
- Class IV: Long, difficult rapids, powerful irregular waves, large boulders. Not suitable for open canoes.
- Class V: Extremely long, obstructed and violent rapid. Scouting is mandatory and rescue difficult. Ability to do Eskimo roll compulsory.
- Class VI: Class V carried to extremes. For teams of experts only.

Distance A measurement of the distance between the access and egress points shown for the trip.

Time A very rough estimate of the time required between the access and egress points shown. The size of the party and the frequency of the portages will have a greater bearing on the time required than the distance or the difficulty of the river. Experience is your best guide and always remember that the joy is in the journey.

Access Directions are given to the usual starting point. Parking is noted if appropriate.

Egress The usual finishing point of a route. As the majority of these trips are one way a car shuttle is required unless you choose to fly in and out. Where the river described is a tributary of a second river, the distance to the next egress point on the second river is noted.

Map The numbers refer to the National Topographic Series 1:50,000 scale maps. The map numbers follow the river course from its source in Manitoba to the mouth so they are not in sequence, but this system makes it easier to select the maps needed.

Season Not all rivers are canoeable all summer. This is a guide to when the river is usually canoeable with a suggestion as to the best time of year for each river.

Author on the Pinawa Channel. Photo: Gerry Reckseidler.

Assiniboine River

Type Large pastoral flatwater river
Difficulty Beginner
Distance 125 km
Time 3-5 days
Access Bridge on Hwy. #340. Park on NE side.
Egress Bridge on Hwy. #34. Wayside park on NE side.
Topo Maps 62G10, 62G11, 62G12, 62G15
Other Maps Assiniboine River Journey of the S.S. Alpha
Season May to September

From the Saskatchewan border to the confluence with the Red River, the Assiniboine meanders placidly for 850 kilometres along the bottom of a once mighty glacial river. Past spacious grainfields, placid cows and busy cityscapes, the Assiniboine flows from the eastern uplands across the broad, sandy shoreline of glacial Lake Agassiz into the billiard table expanse of the Red River Plain. Upstream of the recommended put-in the countryside is largely agricultural. From Portage la Prairie to Winnipeg the river has been extensively diked to prevent flooding. The recommended section of the river flows through the Assiniboine Corridor Wildlife Management Area, Shilo military reserve and Spruce Woods Provincial Park. These three preserves protect the river from agricultural development and preserve its historical and natural qualities. The river flows through Manitoba's desert and can be dehydrating on a hot summer's day. The Assiniboine water is not suitable for drinking, so carry ample water and refill at the springs found along the river.

Spruce Woods Park.

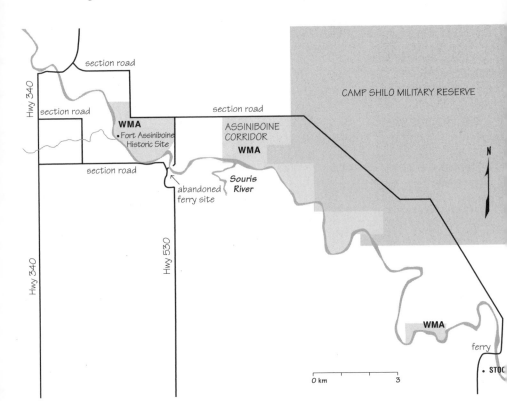

The put-in can be confusing because when the bridge was built, the highway was moved one mile west from the location shown on the topographical map.

Shortly after departing the put-in, watch for a creek coming in on the right. The North West Co. and the Hudson's Bay Co. both had fur trade posts here about 1800, the Bay on the left and the Nor'Westers on the right. These posts were apparently very busy as they are mentioned in several memoirs from that era. A narrow path leads from the river to a clearing where the HBC post, Fort Assiniboine, once stood.

Continuing down river, a commemorative plaque marks the site of the abandoned Treesbank ferry. A small campsite can be found on the left shore.

In two more kilometres the Souris River is reached. Located on the left bank is the Assiniboine Ecological Reserve protecting a mixed-grass prairie.

Scale the 4.5 metre-high banks and stroll among the bluestem and porcupine grasses. In the spring look for crocus and three-flowered avens.

From the Souris River confluence to Stockton ferry, a distance of 19 kilometres, the river skirts the border of Shilo military reserve. Be prepared for cannon fire as the army practises war games. In many places, Shilo's boundaries extend to the river, so landing should be restricted to the right side of the river to insure that you are not trespassing on the reserve. The military mind is excessively paranoid and takes a dim view of trespassing. The Stockton ferry is the last operating ferry in Manitoba. Lunch at the ferry site where a picnic table is conveniently located by the water's edge.

Follow the meanders, past river-washed sandbars and neck-bending cliffs, for 33 kilometres to Hwy. #5 and

Spirit Sands dunes.

Spruce Woods Provincial Park. In times of low water there are several turbulent stretches but no rapids and more importantly no rocks! Watch for a sign indicating the trail to the Devil's Punch Bowl about three kilometres before Hwy. #5 bridge. A must see, the Punch Bowl is a cool, green, sunken pond surrounded by towering spruce trees. Follow the trail inland for a fascinating four kilometre loop through Manitoba's desert and climb a sand dune before returning to your canoes.

Past the bridge there is a full-service campground, but keep paddling around the bend to find the canoe campground and put-in. It is an excellent place to start a day trip or spend the night. The showers in the campground are especially pleasant after a hot day on the river. Visit the

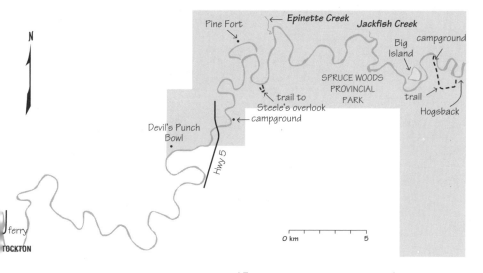

Assiniboine River in very early spring. Note snow.

Remains of the S.S. Alpha.

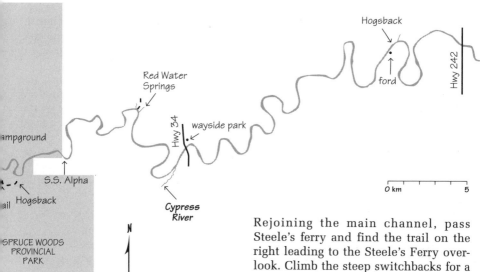

Pine Fort commemorative plaque in the campground to learn about the history of the North West Co. fort located five kilometres downstream.

Through Spruce Woods Provincial Park, the river meanders even more as if reluctant to leave the peacefulness of the park with its clean sandy shores for muddy banks characteristic of the Red River Plain. There is one more established campground about halfway to Hwy. #34. Not as luxurious as the first, it still has tables, privies and water plus a horse corral as the campground is also used by trail riders. With the many level sandbars, camping is never a problem.

Five kilometres from the first campground the river has formed an oxbow. Follow the old channel, if possible, to the site of Pine Fort on a bluff overlooking the river. The North West Co. had a thriving fur trade post here from 1768 to 1793—an exceptionally long-lived establishment by area standards. Nothing remains at the site but the commanding views of the river that must have attracted the original traders.

Rejoining the main channel, pass Steele's ferry and find the trail on the right leading to the Steele's Ferry overlook. Climb the steep switchbacks for a perspective of the distance travelled and an overview of the river ahead.

Returning to the canoes, drift along the river for 15 kilometres to find a small creek coming in on the left. This is Jackfish Creek and leads to Jackfish cabin, an overnight cabin used by cross-country skiers. After Jackfish, the river is shallower for the next 10 kilometres with frequent sandbars to run aground on or to serve as secluded campsites.

The second established campsite is located on river right about five kilometres past Big Island. As mentioned, this is a well-equipped site but intended as a multi-use site. If occupied, a sandbar across the river makes a super substitute. Time permitting, hike the campsite access trail to the service road and follow the road east (left) to the Hogsback. The Hogsback is a high, narrow ridge of sand left by glaciers. When viewed from the river it appears like the back of a hog.

Proceeding downriver, admire the Hogsback from the comfort of your canoe. About two kilometres from the Hogsback, watch for the remains of the S.S. Alpha on river right. The Alpha was a steamboat that plied the Assiniboine between Winnipeg and Fort Ellice (near present-day St. Lazare) from 1875-1885. It met its demise when it ran aground on a sandbar and was abandoned. All that remains are a few hull timbers that are only visible when the water is low. Considering the frequency with which my canoe seems to run aground in these shallow waters, it is a wonder that the Alpha lasted 10 years before being marooned.

Navigate through another series of sandbars and look for a high sand cliff on river left where two intermittent creeks are shown on the map. This creek is known as Red Water Springs. If you are lucky, a stairway leading to the top will still remain. The summit is a narrow, flat peninsula ideal for eating lunch and napping in the afternoon sun. Inland there is a series of trails and a large, permanent youth camp.

The trip from Red Water to the take-out at Hwy. #34 is only about two hours. At Hwy. #34 there is a wayside park on the northeast side of the bridge with a good landing for the canoes. It is possible to continue, for another 30 kilometres, to the ford at Hwy. #350 north of Treherne or even to the bridge at Hwy. #242 before the river leaves the sand hills behind.

Couscous and Chicken

The sand bars and dunes on the Assiniboine River remind me of the Sahara. This Mediterranean dish enhances the atmosphere.

Servings: 4
4 oz chicken, dried
2 oz dried vegetable flakes
1 tb oil
1 ts salt
1/8 cup raisins
1 pinch chicken seasoning
1 pinch orange Kool-Aid for colour
9 oz couscous
2 tb margarine

Rehydrate the chicken and vegetables. Add all the ingredients except the couscous to 1-1/2 cups of water and bring to a boil. Stir in the couscous. Remove from the heat and let stand for 2 minutes. Add the margarine and cook for 3 minutes over medium heat.

Berens River

Type Large wilderness whitewater river
Difficulty Intermediate
Distance 148 km
Time 5-8 days
Access By plane to Little Grand Rapids on Family Lake.
Egress By plane or boat from Berens River Indian Reserve.
Topo Maps 53D3, 53D4, 63A1, 63A2, 63A6, 63A7
Other Maps *Bucky's RiverRunner Guide*, Berard's Little Grand Rapids Routes
Season May to September

The Berens River has the largest catchment area of all rivers flowing into the east side of Lake Winnipeg and therefore it is canoeable until late fall. This long season and relatively easy upstream travel made the Berens the principal route used by aboriginals and fur-traders travelling between James Bay and the interior of Manitoba. Perhaps because of its long history, there are more named rapids on the Berens than on other rivers in Manitoba.

The Berens is unusual in that it often divides into several channels, creating many possible variations for a journey down the river. There are many waterfalls requiring only short portages and few runnable rapids, which is why it was the favoured route of the fur traders. Much of the shoreline has been burned in recent years and one long stretch of marsh is a visually unappealing panorama.

From Little Grand Rapids follow the southern shore of Family Lake westward 12 kilometres to Night Owl Lake. The right channel is the preferred route into Night Owl Lake. Thread your way through the maze of islands in Night Owl to the portage hidden in the nondescript left channel. If you see Night Owl Falls you have missed the turn and have to retrace your course. It is possible to portage at the falls but very difficult owing to the

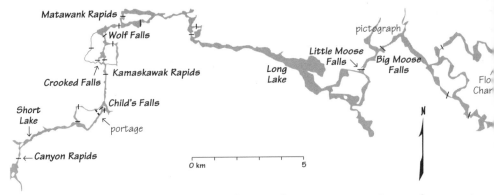

deadfall from a recent fire. Unfortunately, this long portage (520 paces) provides no views of the spectacular seven metre-high falls. These striking falls are worth a short detour. From the end of the portage, paddle across to the small falls on your left. Portage above these falls and paddle around the corner to view the main falls.

After viewing the falls, continue down the river past the class I-II rapid at Whiteman Falls and enter a short, unburned section. Crane Falls, another 3.5 kilometres, is a three metre-high waterfall with a portage across the centre of the island in the middle of the river. There is a good campsite on the south side of the big island at the entrance to Horseshoe Lake

and numerous campsites on the many islands of Horseshoe Lake.

The class I Manitou Rapids divides the two halves of Horseshoe Lake. Hike to the top of the rock here for a commanding view of Horseshoe Lake and Manitou Rapids.

Leaving Manitou Rapids, either channel is suitable. Flour Channel on the right is perhaps a little longer but more scenic and has a pictograph at the entrance. Both channels have portages at the falls but the left channel also has two class I rapids.

Stop and examine the pictograph on river right about 30 metres before Big Moose Falls. This pictograph is reputed to reward those who leave an offering with a successful hunt. It also seems to

Pictograph at Big Moose Falls.

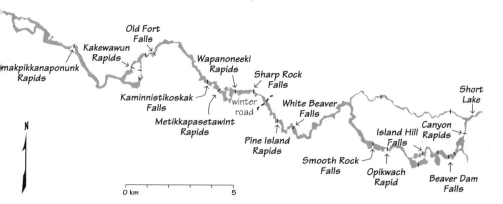

work for running rapids. At Big Moose Rapids the river is divided by an island with the portage in a small bay on river left immediately before the left channel. Located on the right channel is a fine, level campsite from which both channels are visible as is the undercut rock face that makes running the three metre-high falls dangerous.

It is 1.5 kilometres to Little Moose Falls, the last rapid before Long Lake. Take the right channel at Little Moose and run the 0.3 metre ledge or line the canoe over on river left. The river divides at the end of the rapid and flows around a big island before entering Long Lake. The right channel is the more direct route to Long Lake.

Relax and enjoy the easy seven kilometre paddle down this long, narrow lake. Look for the water survey station on the left side which owing to budget restraints this station has been discontinued. The cable stretched across the river at the narrows near the end of the lake was used to take current readings.

Past Matawank Rapids the river divides into three channels of which the centre is usually the easiest. Wolf Falls is a double set with the second being a small ledge. There is a large campsite at Wolf Falls and also one in the left channel. Between Wolf and Crooked falls stay on the right shore. This channel leads to a double fall that must be lined on river right as the new growth after the 1980 fire has obliterated the old portage.

The three branches of the river rejoin at Crooked Falls, creating some difficult cross currents that have to be run in loaded canoes. Following immediately after Crooked Falls is Kamaskawak Rapids, a short class I-II that can be run either side of the island. Child's Falls, the last rapid in this section, is about 1.5 kilometres downstream. Typically, the Berens divides into four branches. There is a good portage on river right of the farthest right channel. Alternatively, the right channel can be used but there is rarely enough water and the two rapids in this channel are often boulder gardens that must be waded. The two channels on the left lead to waterfalls and are not recommended.

After Child's Falls there is five kilometres of flatwater paddling before the river again separates into two channels. This time the left is the preferred route. Although longer, it is much more scenic, has higher flow and has many more rapids, albeit the majority requiring portaging. The first rapid in this series is Canyon Rapids, a class III-IV with a ledge and keeper at the end. The portage is on river left behind the rock in the bay above the rapid. Besides being hard to find, the portage is overgrown, indicating little use perhaps because the ravine it follows for its entire length cannot be seen from the river.

Keeping to the right of the islands, run a class I- at the narrows above Beaver Dam Falls and then portage 50 paces across the island at Beaver Dam. There is a good campsite on the island. The right side of Beaver Dam is a class I-II and the left is a ledge.

There is a discrepancy between the topographical map and Berard's Little Grand Rapids Routes map at this point. Beaver Dam Falls on the topographical map is indicated as BR20 on the Canoe Route map and BR21 is shown as Beaver Dam Falls.

The next falls just around the corner is a mélange of small, low-lying islands any of which can be used to portage the falls. The many small islands here can be confusing, so check the map carefully before proceeding to Island Hill Falls. Keep to the right side to avoid the main channel to Island Hill Falls. Run the small rapid at the head of the right channel and quickly eddy out right to find the portage. This short portage ends at the base of the falls. Run a class I rapid on either side of the small island where the river rejoins the main channel below Island Hill Falls. The next rapid, Opikwach, which is a class II-III, can be lined or a short portage can be made on river left.

The final rapid in this series is Smooth Rock Falls, a class III with a short portage and a small campsite on river right, the first site since Beaver Dam Falls. After Smooth Rock Falls try spotting the weedy mouth of the north channel. Congratulate yourself on choosing the correct channel for once.

At White Beaver Falls the river drops about 3.6 metres over three ledges, making for great photographs. The falls are hidden by a long, thin spire of rock lying across the river. A 50 pace portage on river right goes around all three ledges. Pine Island Rapids is reached after a brief paddle. This class I-II can be run on river left of the left channel.

Downstream of Pine Island Rapids the main winter road, serving the communities on the east side of Lake Winnipeg, crosses the river. The location is marked by the remains of a bridge. Years ago bridges were built at river crossings, but unsurprisingly they were destroyed by ice. Although no longer in use, the bridge is apparently too expensive to remove or destroy. If mosquitoes have been a problem, this is a breezy spot for lunch.

Use the left channel and portage across the island avoiding Sharp Rock Falls, a class III-IV ledge. This is the start of a seven kilometre section with seven falls or rapids. The portage at Wapanoneeki can be hard to find as it is at the head of the bay on river right on the corner before the rapid. As Wapanoneeki is a double set with the lower being a class III-IV at high water, it is comforting to know where the por-

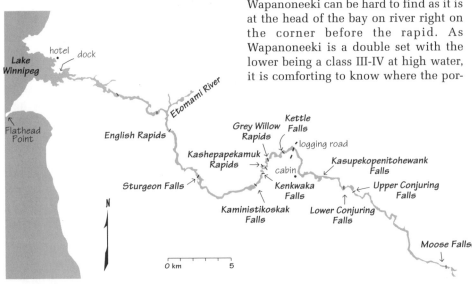

tage is if needed. Metikkapasetawint Rapids is a lift-over on river left and at Kaminnistikoskak Falls there is a short portage also on river left past this ledge. From here to Old Fort Falls there is lots of fast water but no rapids.

Old Fort Falls presents a dilemma. The choice is a 150-pace portage on river right through a recent burn with some deadfall or a 50-pace portage on river left through a very dense stand of young pine. A third option, if you are confident of your paddling skills, is to run the upper part and line the ledge at the end of the rapid. The last rapid in this section, like the first, is a ledge that requires a short portage on river left.

Past this rapid the river again separates into two channels. There are two rapids in the left channel: the first is a class II-III with no known portage; the second is a ledge with a portage on river left. Kakewawun Rapids, in the right channel, has a three metre drop. The easiest portage is across the left island. Both channels have small campsites, at Kakewawun Rapids and on the island between the rapids in the left channel.

Beyond Kakewawun Rapids the shoreline becomes low with alder and willow predominating until Asamapikkanaponunk Rapids, a class I. Here the burn is finally left behind and you enter the mixed-wood forests and granite outcrops typical of the Shield.

The river soon narrows and rushes over three metre-high Moose Falls, quickly followed by a class I rapid. A 400-pace portage on river right begins by climbing a steep clay bank, then goes through dense bush for the remainder of the route. The start is difficult to locate, but once found the portage is easy to follow. On river left a more difficult 250-pace portage through the burn comes out at the base of the falls and the lower rapids are run. Choose the left side if it is your turn to carry the packs rather than the canoe. It is 11.5 kilometres to Upper Conjuring Falls, the longest stretch of flatwater since Long Lake. Un-

fortunately, this quiet and pretty stretch shows evidence of clear-cut logging.

Upper Conjuring Falls is a class V waterfall preceded by a class I+ rapid. A 300-pace portage on river left is well used but the clear-cut comes within 10 metres of the portage. A second portage can be found by running the upper rapid and ferrying out right before the waterfall. A small campsite, the first since Kakewawun Rapids, and a swimming hole beside the rapid is inviting on a hot day.

Lower Conjuring Falls around the corner is another three metre-high fall with a short portage on river left. The portage ends at a strong eddy that is often filled with debris, making the put-in difficult. Leaving the eddy, usually a delicate operation, ferry across the base of the falls to regain the main current. Conjuring up a bit of magic to remain upright would be fitting. (No wonder this place is called Conjuring Falls!) Kasupekopenitohewank Falls is next, a class I-II with a short portage on river right.

In the next five kilometres of paddling you pass a trapper's cabin and a logging camp. A barge tied to the shore at the logging camp is used to move vehicles across the river. A road parallels the river from the camp to the town of Berens River. There are frequent signs of human activity on the river between the logging camp and the town, but also some of the most intriguing rapids to run.

At Kettle Falls, the beginning of the last section, the river divides into five channels, all of them very rocky. There are several portages depending on how far down the rapid you can paddle before your canoe becomes stuck on the rocks. The best portage is on the island on the left side of the river, but it is also the longest.

Grey Willow is a dramatic three metre-high waterfall with many interesting rock formations. Photographers could easily waste a roll of film here. It is surprising how much one rock looks like another on a slide at home! The portage is on the left side of the right-hand is-

Night Owl Falls.

Manitou Rapids.

land at a small notch in the rock. It is an easy 50 paces all downhill and there is a decent campsite at the end, but the roar of the falls makes conversation difficult.

The right or main channel is the best route at Kashepapekamuk Rapids. This is a double with a large pool separating the class I upper set from the lower ledge. The ledge can be run or you can use the easy lift-over on river left. Climb the high rock on river left above the ledge to get a bird's-eye view of canoes shooting the rapids.

Around the corner is Kenkwaka Falls where the full flow of the river is forced through a narrow gap. Depending on the flow, this rapid can range from class I to class IV. A 120-pace portage on river left affords an excellent view of the entire rapid.

Located a kilometre downstream is Kaminnistikoskak Falls, the last rapid in this section. It is a class II-III with a short portage on river left.

It is another five kilometres to Sturgeon Falls, the last portage on the river. An unnamed class I-II about 200 metres before Sturgeon can be portaged on river left of the left channel where the river falls about 1.5 metres over a ledge. The right channel has two ledges and is runnable under suitable conditions. Sturgeon Falls is a 3.6 metre-high waterfall. The 150-pace portage is on river left of the left-hand channel. The name suggests that this would be a good place to fish, and it certainly appears to be well used.

The last rapid shown on the map is English Rapids, a wide, easy class I with a short portage on river right. There are two more class I rapids at the narrows past the Etomami River junction.

The town of Berens River has grown considerably since the map was printed, and it extends much farther upriver than shown on the map. A bridge has been built across the river. Continue paddling through the town and at Kasepeskisewekak Point turn right and head for the government dock across the bay. The hotel and airport are up the road; the RCMP station is at the end of the dock on the left and the Northern store's manager's house on the right. The manager will store your canoe until transportation for it can be arranged back to Winnipeg.

One Pot Dhal

A trip on the Berens River with a group of vegetarians challenged my culinary skills. This recipe was a hit with both vegetarians and carnivores alike.

Servings: 4
3/4 package red lentils
2 sm garlic cloves
1 sm carrot
1 package peas, dried
1 sm zucchini
1 sm onion
2 ts curry powder
4 oz cheese

Soak the lentils in 4 cups of water for 4 hours. Add the vegetables to the water and bring to a boil. Cook until the lentils are soggy. Add curry to taste. Serve topped with cheese.

Bird River

Type Mid-sized semi-wilderness flatwater river
Difficulty Intermediate
Distance 34 km
Time 1 day
Access Boat launch at east end of Bird Lake off Hwy. #315.
Egress Campground half a km past Hwy. #315 bridge.
Topo Maps 52L5 and 52L6
Other Maps Berard's Oiseau-Manigotagan Routes
Season May to September

The Bird River drains a low swampy area of Nopiming Provincial Park where the shoreline is often flat and densely covered with alder and willow. There are few camping sites, or even lunch spots, along the river. Hwy. #315 and the Bernic Lake Road parallel the river over much of its distance, so traffic noise can be a distraction. The traffic has accustomed the wildlife to human activity and therefore wildlife viewing is better than along other more remote rivers. The river falls about 15 metres from Bird Lake to Lac du Bonnet. However, most of this drop occurs near the finish in two waterfalls and one long rapid. For most of its length the Bird is a placid, slow-moving river that is canoeable from early spring to late fall. The river attracts an abundance of birds, especially ducks. Eagles, osprey, herons and kingfishers are also common along the river.

In the early seventies a survey discovered 44 archaeological sites along this short section of the river. Material recovered from these sites ranges from stone tools to metal buckles, indicating long use of the river by many different cultures.

The first eight kilometres of this trip from Tulabi Falls to the river mouth is along the heavily developed shores of Bird Lake. It is an additional three kilometres to Hwy. #315, an alternate start-

Seff and Dave Hunt near Shatford Creek.

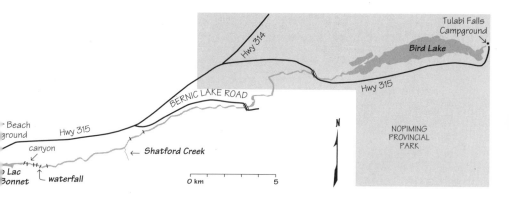

ing point if you choose not to paddle the lake, with its cottages and motorboats. There is a large wayside park and an excellent boat launch on the northwest side of the bridge. However, no overnight camping is permitted.

The first rapid is six kilometres downstream from Hwy. #315. It is a ledge with a 0.3 metre drop. A short portage crashes through the bush on river left. From here the Bernic Lake Road is visible. This is a private road leading to the Bernic Lake tantalum mine and crosses the river six kilometres downstream from Hwy. #315. The substantial concrete arch bridge hides the beginning of a long class II+ rapid with two log jams near the tail that require careful scouting. A 500-pace portage on river left along a bush road paralleling the river is a safer alternative.

The river resumes its placid course for the next six kilometres until a class I rapid is encountered. Easy access to the Bernic Lake Road makes this rapid a popular fishing and camping spot. From here it is only 10 kilometres downstream to Hwy. #315. This is a pleasant day trip with the option of biking back to the starting point.

Located another kilometre downstream is a major rapid with a six metre-high waterfall in the middle. Portage river left 300 paces along a well-travelled but poorly maintained trail.

A short way downstream watch for Shatford Creek entering on the left. In the spring this is a very picturesque waterfall. Climb the hill beside Shatford Creek for an overlook of the extensive swamp that is the source of the creek.

Continuing down the river, pass an old trailer, and after six kilometres of quiet paddling you encounter a short class I rapid that can be run at most water levels. Another 1.5 kilometres farther on there is a three metre-high waterfall. The 400-pace portage is on river right at the lip of the falls and up a very steep rock face. Use extreme caution when landing the canoe. The portage circles a small bay to an equally steep put-in on the far side. Watch for prickly pear cactus growing alongside the trail. From the waterfall the next rapid is visible. This rapid can be run but you must ferry out right, before the large rock, and into the bay to avoid going down the canyon. The canyon is an impressive sight, especially in the early spring with snow clinging to the sides and the water surging through the narrow passage. The canyon is a sinuous class III+ rapid with a large log jam near the end. The 1000-pace portage on river right follows a rock ridge along the canyon edge about halfway, then drops off the ridge to follow an all terrain vehicle (ATV) trail. The ATV trail makes for easy walking but is usually wet. Leave the ATV trail and return to the river where the trail turns right and climbs a steep hill.

The final rapid is just around the bend. The upper section is a class I+ and can be run at most water levels. A

Below the canyon in low water.

Portaging the waterfall.

road coming in from the right marks the transition between the upper and middle section. Take-out at the road to scout the next section. The middle section is a class II+ rapid with many large boulders. Unfortunately, the portage ends before the rapid does and the last 30 metres must be run. The put-in is difficult at high water levels and there is a large standing wave at the end of the rapid. The road found between the upper and lower section leads to Hwy. #315 after a short walk. It can be used as an alternate egress point, but a trench at the highway prevents vehicle access to the river.

The final rapid in the set and the river is a class I that leads into a lake. It is an easy paddle down the lakeshore past many cottages to the bridge on Hwy. #315. Past the bridge, Pioneer Beach Campground has a small beach that is suitable for a take-out. In former years they have been willing to guard our bicycles while we canoed the river.

Canoe Scramble

This is a hearty breakfast to prepare you for the many portages found on the Bird River.

Servings: 4

6 oz bacon bar or salami
8 oz cheddar cheese
2 pkg dried hashbrowns with onions
4 tb butter

Rehydrate the potatoes. Drain, place in an oiled fry pan and stir until slightly browned. Add the bacon bar or salami and continue browning. Melt cheese over top.

Black River

Type Small wilderness river with many technical rapids
Difficulty Intermediate
Distance 95 km
Time 4-5 days
Access Boat launch at Black Lake Provincial Campground in Nopiming Provincial Park.
Egress Bridge on Hwy. #304, 40 km north of Pine Falls.
Park at wayside park on NW side of bridge.
Topo Maps 52L11, 52L12, 52L13 and 62I16
Other Maps Berard's Oiseau-Manigotagan Routes
Season April to May

The Black River originates in Black Lake on the Manitoba-Ontario border and flows for 95 kilometres through the mixed woodland forest of the Precambrian Shield in eastern Manitoba before eventually discharging into Lake Winnipeg. Because of its length, short season and inaccessibility it is seldom paddled by recreational canoeists and therefore offers a wilderness experience not available on more heavily used rivers such as the Manigotagan and Bloodvein. Ducks and geese are abundant, songbirds are common and it is not unusual to see woodland caribou, moose, otter, beaver and mink. There are many picturesque little waterfalls and rapids, mainly class II and III. The portages are often hard to find or nonexistent. Good campsites are infrequent and there are several long stretches through marshes where there are no campsites at all.

Deadfall.

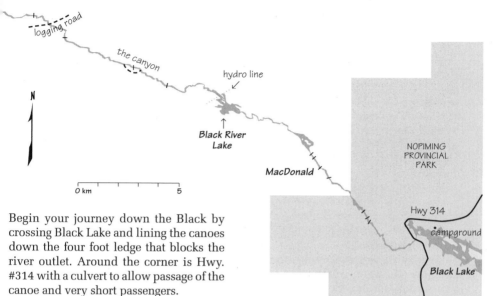

Begin your journey down the Black by crossing Black Lake and lining the canoes down the four foot ledge that blocks the river outlet. Around the corner is Hwy. #314 with a culvert to allow passage of the canoe and very short passengers.

The first four kilometres of the Black consist of a large swamp. If the river is high you can paddle across the meanders, otherwise you have to follow the torturous main channel. Canada Geese, Northern Harriers and hundreds of red-winged blackbirds with their brilliant scarlet wing patches live in the swamp. The river exits the swamp via a narrow class IV rapid located in the granite ridge that borders the swamp.

Leaving this rapid, the topography changes and for the next eight kilometres there are 10 rocky rapids and several small lakes. Most of the rapids are straightforward, but halfway between the two small unnamed lakes there is a deceiving double rapid that I call MacDonald after the famous detective writer. Since the portage doesn't lead to the obvious put-in after the first rapid, some investigation is in order. A quick search reveals a second rapid, hidden by a sharp bend, that is a class IV with a two metre-high waterfall followed by three quick sharp bends in the river. Lacking an established path around the waterfall, it is prudent and fastest to use the long 600-pace portage around both

sets. It is again low lying and swampy for the final four kilometres to Black River Lake where a three foot ledge blocks the entrance to the lake. After all the swamp paddled through, the lake itself is a pleasant surprise. The shoreline is rock and there are several good islands for camping. Halfway down the lake pass under the hydro line supplying power to the communities of Bissett and Manigotagan.

At the west end of the lake there is a nine metre-high waterfall. To the right is a short, extremely steep portage to the pool below the falls. The river exits the pool by slamming into a rock wall, turning 90 degrees and dropping over a ledge. On the left are two very steep, heavily wooded ridges with no defined portage, but this route avoids both the waterfall and ledge and leads to an easy put-in. As usual, both choices are bad.

After the lake, the river resumes its meandering course through the swamp for the next 10 kilometres. There are three short rapids, all class I. This part of the river is on the migration route of the Owl Lake herd, one of the most southerly herds of woodland caribou. Drifting quietly downstream in the early morning maximizes the chance of spotting caribou.

Every river has a rapid called "the canyon" and the Black is no exception. The canyon divides the upper swampy section of the Black from the mixed woodlands of the lower section. Located 10 kilometres from Black River Lake, it is a class II rapid with a canoe swamping standing wave immediately preceding a sharp left turn, followed, of course, by a rock garden. The portage is hidden in a small bay on river left. Skirting the edge of the canyon, the portage gives an excellent view of the rapid and has great photo opportunities.

Luckily there are six kilometres of flatwater paddling to the next rapid, giving your clothing a chance to dry. A ledge at the top of the next rapid can be lined on river right and the remainder of this class II run. The rapid ends in a magnificent little pool surrounded by high rock walls. At the far end of the pool, a portage is necessary to avoid the 2.5 metre-high falls, or alternatively there is a long portage, on the right, around both the rapid and falls. There is a large, level campsite adjacent to the portage, the first good site since leaving Black River Lake.

Shortly after leaving the falls, a logging camp on the riverbank is passed. This concentration of industrial machinery is an incongruous sight on the banks of an otherwise pristine wilderness river. Next to the camp a logging road crosses the river. Here the river runs through a culvert, then makes three sharp turns in quick succession, each with a class I rapid often congested with debris from logging operations.

After the logging camp, the river becomes constricted and the forest becomes predominantly oak and black ash. For the next 25 kilometres, the overhanging trees can make this section a very dark and sombre place. When the sun is shining, it is a place of magic and intriguing shadows. There are numerous rapids and small waterfalls in this

Sharon Macdonald and author enjoying a quiet moment. Photo: Roger Turenne.

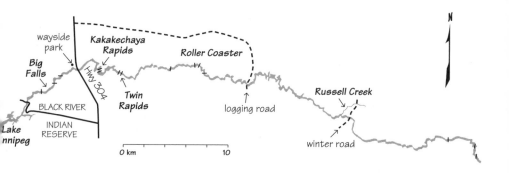

section. Campsites are scarce with the best ones customarily at the waterfalls, which usually offer good fishing. Typically, the rapids are preceded by a small ledge that requires lining. The remainder of the rapid is often runnable, but can be very technical owing to the confining banks.

Finally, the only landmark on this portion of the river, the old winter freighting road from Pine Falls to Bissett, comes into view, reassuring you of your position. An immense logjam, the first of many, is also located at the road. In a clearing beside the road is the remains of an old cabin. The skeletal shapes of several other buildings can be found nearby. The artifacts found nearby suggest the site was occupied in the 1960s. The large site and various buildings suggest this was once a logging camp.

The last of the rapids in this section are located three kilometres past the winter road. There is an undistinguished set of four that except for the first and last normally require portages. The next 12 kilometres are through mixed woodlands with a low, wet shoreline and no campsites. Beavers, otters and moose are common. Unfortunately, beaver dams and logjams are also common. Many of these logjams have been established long enough to grow their own lawns. Allow half a day to drag, haul, lift and push your canoe across these 12 kilometres.

A wooden logging bridge spanning a rapid signals the end of logjams and a return to the rocky outcrops typical of the Shield. From here to the mouth, the campsites are much better and more frequent. Real Berard describes this rapid on his map as "a beautiful spot for camping and resting." Unfortunately, the bridge mars the beauty of the spot. It is still a good campsite and can be peaceful if the logging road is not being used.

When the bridge was built, a very wide swath was cleared and much of the debris has wound up in the river. This debris and the bridge piers make this a difficult rapid, but the alternative is a long portage. The bridge is about one day's paddle upstream of Lake Winnipeg and begins the best section of the Black for rapids. There are many class II and III rapids interspersed with a few class I's. Some of the more memorable ones are the class II-III rapids a few paddle strokes past the bridge, with a short portage on river left if you decide against running this rapid. Half a kilometre farther the river turns sharp left into a tricky class II that can be run river left. There is a low, wide rock at the top of the rapid causing logjams and obstructing the narrow channel leading to the rapid. There is a portage on river right over a high rock with a good campsite on top.

An unmarked rapid, known as Roller Coaster, is the most challenging along this section. It is a class III where the river drops 1.2 metres through a very narrow vee just wide enough to pass a single canoe. A low shelving rock on the

Typical Black River campsite.

Jeannine Macaulay and Bill Kocay at Roller Coaster Rapids.

right gives your companions the opportunity to scrutinize your technique at close range and get some superb pictures of your canoe disappearing into the curling wave. An excellent place for lunch is beside the cool rushing water while you psych yourself up to run the rapid.

Twin Rapids is portaged on river right and followed by Kakakechaya Rapids, the last marked rapid, which is a double waterfall. The first is 2.5 metres portaged on river left. The second is six metres portaged on river right. This portage is short and very steep and the put-in is immediately at the base of the falls. Launching your canoe directly into the

thundering falls is a damp but exhilarating experience, especially when there are logs or overhanging branches to contend with.

It's 3.5 kilometres from Kakakechaya Rapids to Hwy. #304, and there is a final class I under the bridge to the take-out at the Black River wayside park. Alternatively, you can continue another eight kilometres to Lake Winnipeg and finish at the Black River Indian Reserve. There are six more rapids before the lake, all of them easy class I's except the last, Big Falls, which as you can guess is a big waterfall with lots of open rock for picnicking or swimming.

Black Bean Soup

During one early season outing on the Black River this spicy soup banished the cold and brought tears to our eyes if we accidentally bit into a chili. It is a meal in a bowl!

Servings: 4
6 tb cilantro
1 sm onion
1 sm red pepper
1 sm green pepper
1 dash cayenne pepper
1 tb oil
2 dried chillies
1 bay leaf
1 lemon
1 can tomatoes (or a dozen sun-dried tomatoes and 1 can tomato paste)
2 cups black bean flakes (available at health food stores)
1 pkg sour cream mix (optional)
At home, chop and dry the cilantro, onion and peppers. Package. Repack the tomatoes into a sealed container if you don't want to carry cans, or substitute a dozen sun-dried tomatoes and 1 can of tomato paste.

At camp, add the tomatoes to 1-1/2 cups of water and bring to a boil. Sauté the onion and peppers with 1 tb oil until the onion is clear. Add the onion, peppers and remaining ingredients, except the lemon, to the tomatoes; stir briefly. Simmer, covered, on medium heat for 5 minutes. Stir and serve. Best with bannock and garnished with a slice of lemon or a dollop of sour cream.

Bloodvein River

Type Large wilderness whitewater river
Difficulty Beginner
Distance 205 km
Time 7-12 days
Access By plane to Artery Lake or by canoe from Wallace Lake via Siderock Lake and the Obukowin and Ford portages.
Egress At Bloodvein Indian Reserve. There is a daily ferry service (except weekends and holidays) to Hwy. #234. Vehicles can be cached at "the Scotchman's," the second last house before the ferry dock.
Topo Maps 52M5, 52M6, 52M12, 62P8, 62P9, 62P10, 62P15
Other Maps *Bucky's RiverRunner Guide*, Berard's Sasaginnigak and Kautunigan Routes
Season May to September

The Bloodvein, Manitoba's first Heritage River, is a canoeist's paradise. Effortless paddling and easy portages make the spectacular scenery on this wilderness river accessible to even the novice paddler.

The headwaters of the Bloodvein are near Red Lake, Ontario, and the only access is by canoe or float plane. Starting from Red Lake requires crossing a large, open lake followed by a long, difficult portage through an old windblown burn to Knox Lake on the Bloodvein. Because of the challenges of this route, most canoeists choose to fly into Artery Lake.

From Knox Lake to the Manitoba border the Bloodvein is a series of large lakes strung together by the river. Entering Manitoba and Atikaki Provincial Wilderness Park, the river flows for 205 kilometres through a series of narrow channels and small lakes into Lake Winnipeg at "the Narrows."

From Knox Lake, the Bloodvein flows through Murdock, Larus, Simeon, Barclay and finally Artery Lake. The two sections of Artery Lake are separated by five kilometres of narrow river channel. This stretch has the largest and best preserved pictograph site in western Canada. The brilliant red images seem to leap out from the grey-green rock walls. The number and diversity of the drawings is startling. The most impressive is the huge buffalo that dominates the centre of the scene. Whoever painted these scenes was obviously familiar with the prairies, hundreds of kilometres to the west. If these images seem familiar, it is because they were featured in the 1993 Canadian Recreational Canoe Association calendar.

*Author at boat roller portage.
Photo: Clyde Cowan.*

A small ledge blocks the exit from Artery Lake. If you choose to portage around the rapid, there is a boat transporter so you can roll your fully-laden canoes across. All portages should be this easy!

The next 15 kilometres are very picturesque. Around every turn the river reveals stunning new vistas as it winds through a narrow channel with a succession of easy rapids and choice campsites. One particularly impressive rock has split leaving a gap of 2.5 metres at the top. According to legend, young Indians would prove their bravery by jumping from one sloping surface to the other. Past the split rock there is a tricky class II-III ledge with a right angle turn that can be run if the canoe is lined up perfectly, otherwise it's swim time.

You soon reach Bushey Lake, which, as the name suggests, is a shallow, weedy lake with mediocre campsites. It is only a short distance to Stonehouse Lake, a magnificent lake with huge cliffs rising straight out of the water. In spite of the abundance of rock, campsites are difficult to find owing in part to the steepness of the shoreline.

Leaving Stonehouse Lake the river enters a narrow canyon where three sets of rapids must be portaged. The middle set is the longest, but a pleasant campsite awaits at the end of the portage. Beyond the last rapid the river widens and flows quickly past high rock walls. The current transports you swiftly to the next rapids—they never seem to be far away on the Bloodvein. There are three major rapids on this section of the Bloodvein, all requiring portaging, the first two on the right and the last on the left. The portages are short but compensate by being steep.

After the last violent rapid, the river widens and the shoreline is gentler. The towering hills are carpeted with dense evergreens from the waterline to the crown. It is relaxing to drift past this canopy of green after passing the stark rock-ribbed country to the east.

A solitary cabin perched high on a hill above the river soon comes into view. It looks very out of place in this wilderness park. It is a fly-in fishing camp and owns the motorboats seen at the previous portage. With luck there

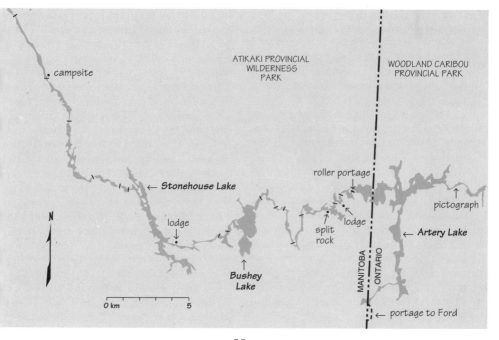

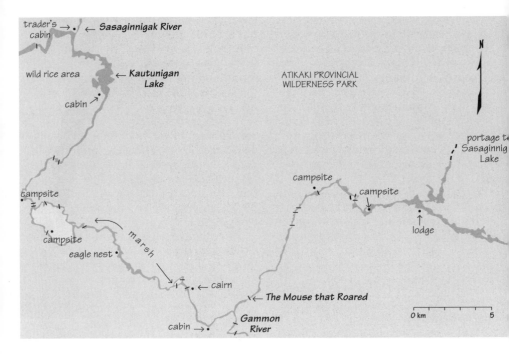

will be no guests staying at the cabin to disturb the quiet of the wilderness with their noisy outboards.

Leaving the cabin behind, there is an excellent campsite located on the small island about a kilometre before the next waterfall. Here a long portage, found in a small bay on river left between the rapid and waterfall, bypasses the next three rapids. Apparently the waterfall and portage are a barrier to the fly-in anglers as there are no boats cached at this portage.

The river again narrows and the next 12 kilometres to the junction of the Gammon River is the most scenic on the Bloodvein. Here the river is deep and fast with five sets of rapids and several excellent campsites with the best on the island at the first rapid. Many rocks and a ledge combine to make the middle rapid a class II-III and an intricate and challenging run. For those readers whose lives are already challenging enough, there is a portage on river right. The last rapid before the Gammon is known as "The Mouse that Roared" because of its terrifying sound and gentle nature.

The Gammon is a popular way to access the Bloodvein and the campsites and portages are more heavily used downstream of the Gammon. About five kilometres past the Gammon a class I-II rapid is located. On the right shore, high above the river, stands a cairn erected in 1925. Beneath the cairn there is a survey marker placed by A. Gammon, after whom the Gammon River is named. This and similar markers served as control points for the first aerial survey ever done in Canada. Yet another superb campsite is located on the left shore.

In another half a kilometre the river divides. The left channel leads to a 1.5 metre-high waterfall. The portage is on river right in a small bay that is hidden from view until the brink is imminent. The wide, flat rock provides ample room to take-out, but the put-in requires paddling hard against a strong back eddy to get into the violent main current at the base of the falls. It is very easy to get turned around and wind up back where you started from, hopefully still upright. On the right channel there are

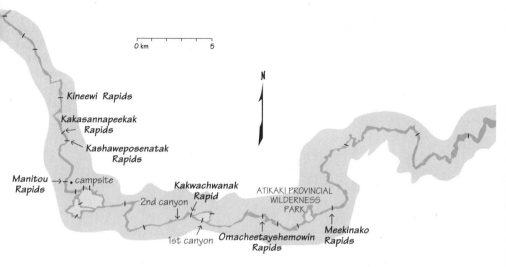

three short, narrow class I-II rapids. There are no portages so these three rapids have to be run or lined.

The next seven kilometres are through a marsh with no campsites. A frequently-occupied bald eagle nest dominates the centre of the marsh. From late spring, the young can be seen demanding food and usually in early August they will begin their first tentative flights. While the adults observe from a more cautious distance, the youngsters sit and watch as canoeists drift past, cameras snapping furiously.

At the end of the marsh there is a class I-II runnable on river right with a short portage on river left, before the river divides around a large island. There are four rapids, two of which require short portages on the right side, but it is easier and more scenic. The first marked rapid requires caution as the clear channel is on river left but the portage is on river right. The more commonly-used left channel is longer but there is only one portage, around a violent class V waterfall. An interesting class I must be run to return to the main channel after the waterfall. The rapid is straightforward, but aligning the canoe properly with the main current to avoid being swept into the rocks is challeng-

ing. There are many good campsites on the left channel with the best located on the portage overlooking the falls.

The two branches of the river rejoin and race toward three more waterfalls in the next five kilometres. The take-outs for these falls are all close to the lip with the middle one having the extra disadvantage of being hidden by an island. This portage goes through a good campsite, which can make the portage difficult to follow because of all the trails radiating from the campsite.

At the last waterfall the portage is only 50 paces with yet another steep entry and exit complicated by being virtually at the brink of the fall. A class I-II is only a few strokes away. This rapid has a short 30-pace portage on river right and surprisingly an easy in and out. From here to Kautunigan Lake it is again marshy and there are no campsites so, if it is close to camp time, this rapid is a good place to stop.

Although there are a few rock faces on the west side, Kautunigan Lake has a low, swampy shoreline. Continuing downstream there are granite headlands interspersed with marsh. Poplar, birch and oak are the predominant trees replacing the jack pine and suggesting a better soil. Wild rice is common along

Jeannine Macaulay and author running a Bloodvein rapid. Photo: Roger Turenne.

Artery Lake pictographs.

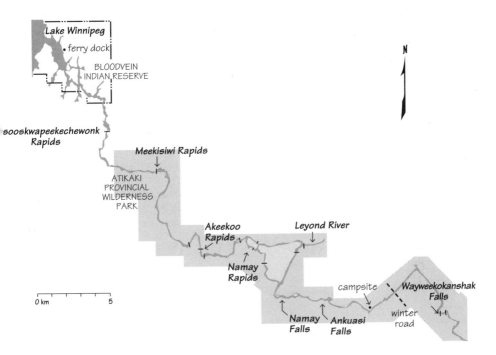

the shore and the remains of a couple of old rice camps are recognizable.

Located at the junction of the Sasaginnigak River is the remains of a cabin of an independent trader who lived here in the thirties. Why don't you examine the artifacts and speculate about who he might have traded with? Was the Bloodvein once a trade route before the coming of the airplanes? Topographical maps from the 1920s show all the portages with the distances given in chains. This would suggest that the Bloodvein was once a well-travelled route. The Hudson's Bay Co. had a post on the Bloodvein in 1794 but its location has been lost. Could it have been here at the junction? It would seem to be a logical spot for a trading post.

Ten kilometres past the Sasaginnigak, the wild rice is left behind and the granite and jack pine that typifies the Precambrian Shield returns. The transition is marked by a class III-IV ledge. The portage is on river right along with a good campsite. Here the river narrows and the current becomes

stronger. There is five kilometres of flatwater paddling to Meekinako Rapids, a rocky class II-III. Now the river becomes very narrow and picturesque as it winds its way through the granite-walled canyon. An abundance of camp-sites can be found on the rocky shore-lines in this area.

The next seven kilometres contain seven rapids, all class I except for the last two, which are known collectively as the Omacheetayshemowin Rapids, both of which can be portaged on river right. Two-and-a-half kilometres past Omacheetayshemowin, the river enters the first small, steep-walled canyon. A well-marked portage on river left fol-lows a ridge about 21 metres above the class III rapid. Although providing a spectacular view, a shorter, easier por-tage much closer to the rapid can be found on river right. This rapid features a unique double curling wave. Two op-posed curling waves meet in the centre to form a flat, smooth surface over the ledge. Will this unique wave-top sup-port an unloaded canoe? I think it is interesting to speculate, and it is something that deserves to be tested at the first opportunity.

The next rapid is Kakwachwanak, less than a kilometre downstream. At this class III the river drops 1.5 metres over three ledges. A 50-pace portage on river right takes you safely around the ledges.

Around the next bend the river enters the second small, steep-sided canyon. There is a class II-III at the head followed by three class I's. A long portage around all four rapids exists, but it is little-used and difficult to follow. The alternative is a difficult-to-find portage past the first rapid, but this commits you to running the next three rapids as the sheer walls preclude portaging. The rapids are not difficult and there is enough distance between them for you to enjoy the beauty of the canyon. A small campsite at the first rapid tempts you to spend some time at this lovely spot.

For the next seven kilometres, the superb scenery continues with only easy rapids to divert your attention. At this point the river divides into three channels. In the centre channel there is only one short portage. Both of the other channels are longer but equally as scenic and have more rapids to run or if absolutely necessary portage.

Kaneesopakayeheewonk Rapids, where the three channels rejoin, is a 1.5 metre-high ledge with a six-pace portage. At six paces this is easily the shortest portage on the Bloodvein, but the vertical drop is a little too much for lining. As the canoe is longer than the portage, launching it is very easy.

Manitou Rapids is next and it has an excellent campsite. The portage is on river right but there is a clear channel on river left of this rapid with only a short back ferry to avoid the logjam and rock wall at the end. The length and manoeuvring required make this one of the most interesting rapids and yet within the capabilities of most canoeists.

Next is Kashaweposenatak Rapids. Although long, the portage on river left is level and picturesque as it curves through the multi-hued greens of an old-growth boreal forest. A shorter, more difficult portage can be found closer to the falls on river right. From the end of the portage, the next rapid, Kakasannapeekak Rapids is visible. With its three ledges, alternating from each shore, it presents an invitation to the canoeist. Can you ferry across the river before being swept over the ledge? A well-used portage suggests that most canoeists decline the invitation.

At Kineewi Rapids, there are three options to choose from. Portage on the right past both sets of rapids and the falls or portage on the left around the upper rapids and falls. The third option is to run the upper rapid and take-out at the waterfall, cutting the right portage in half! This is the preferred choice for owners of heavy canoes. Choosing the right side requires trying to re-enter the main current through a narrow gap be-

Barry Catt and Carol Kristjansson at Split Rock. Photo: Clyde Cowan.

Author and Dean McLeod portaging a ledge. Photo: Clyde Cowan.

tween two substantial boulders and, if successful, avoiding being slammed into a rock face when the river makes a 90 degree turn in 15 metres. All this makes the class I at the end look very tame indeed.

After Kineewi the rapids become less frequent, but the scenery remains as marvellous. A widening of the river gives the opportunity to paddle side by side and share these peaceful moments, or perhaps do some fishing as you glide along.

Wayweekokanshak Falls, in spite of being hidden around a bend, makes its presence known far upstream with a continuous roar. Even the portage follows a ravine, blocking your view of the falls. By scrambling over the rocks it's possible to find a viewpoint above this powerful waterfall. It is tempting to run this straight chute as there are no dangerous rocks and ample room to set up a rescue boat. In an empty canoe and with luck it might be possible to surf through. Besides, there is 10 kilometres to dry out before the next rapid.

A clearing marks the location where the old winter road crosses the Bloodvein. The road has now been relocated to the western edge of the park. Each winter, after freeze up, a road is ploughed from Manigotagan north up the east side of Lake Winnipeg to bring supplies to the communities in the area. All winter long, semitrailers roar along these roads hauling enough supplies to last for a year. A wildlife refuge parallels the road for its entire length.

Half a kilometre past the old winter road there is an excellent campsite, possibly the best on the Bloodvein. Wide, gently sloping rocks leading into a quiet backwater make a swim enticing on a hot day. On the far side of this granite slide the swift rush of water through a narrow opening provides an exciting but safe ride.

Ankuasi Falls is reached soon after passing the winter road. A long, low tongue of rock on river right provides ample landing for the canoes. Slide the canoe over the rock and scoot past the ledge.

The left channel is the best route to Namay Falls. There is usually very little water going over the left side and it is possible to portage along the riverbed. The right channel leads to a class III rapid with a very steep portage. The view from the top of the portage is great but not worth hauling the canoe up for.

About two kilometres past Namay Falls the river splits into two channels. The main flow is northeast to the junction of the Leyond River. The left channel is easily missed as it looks more like a small creek and has very little flow. There are three rapids in this channel that are usually dried up and necessitate portaging or dragging. The last kilometre makes the effort worthwhile as the river flows through some very narrow passages where the river is confined by vertical rock faces. The main channel, while longer and not as scenic, has no portages.

Take the left channel at Namay Rapids. There are three widely spaced ledges here with a short portage at each one. The wide, flat, open rocks provide plenty of room for camping or sunbathing while the more enthusiastic can practise running rapids, exploring and blueberry picking.

Around the corner is Kaokonapeekeekewonk Rapids where a small island divides the river. Use the right channel as there is often insufficient water going down the left channel. Watch for the three "kettles" or glacial swirl holes on the right side of the portage at Akeekoo Rapids. Ride the tongue down and back paddle hard to slip through the gap between the boulder and the ledge and into the quiet water, to avoid the portage on river left. Three easy rapids lead to the final portage on the Bloodvein at Meekisiwi Rapids, a 0.6 metre ledge. There is a wide expanse of flat rock to portage the canoes across.

Atikaki Wilderness Provincial Park ends appropriately at the hydro line west of Meekisiwi Rapids. Leave the park with a vow to return frequently with fervent hope that the wilderness character that makes the park so appealing will not be eroded by any further commercial development.

There are several good campsites between Meekisiwi and Kasooskwapeekechewonk rapids that allow ample time to reach Bloodvein and catch the noon ferry across Lake Winnipeg.

A bright orange water survey station and several channel markers indicate the Bloodvein Indian Reserve is nearby. Follow the right shore through the maze of islands to reach the ferry landing. The free ferry runs daily Monday to Friday throughout the summer.

Author and Dean McLeod squeezing through drop. Photo: Clyde Cowan.

Catfish with Ginger Peach Sauce

Channel catfish are common in the Bloodvein and are a very savoury delicacy when cooked properly. They can be substituted for dried chicken in outdoor cooking. The traditional method of cooking catfish is to roll the fillets in cornmeal and fry in enough oil to float a canoe. This recipe is easier on the cholesterol count. Make up the sauce at home and it will keep well in the cold waters of the Bloodvein until you land the first catfish.

Servings: 2
For Sauce
1 tb butter
1 ts minced ginger
1 can peaches
1 cup peach jam
1 tb catsup
1 tb white vinegar
1/4 ts tabasco sauce
For Fish
4 catfish fillets
1/2 cup flour
1 tb thyme leaves
1 ts salt
1/2 ts black pepper
2 tb oil
1 tb butter
1/2 cup pecans

To make the sauce melt 1 tb butter in a saucepan. Add ginger and stir. Add the canned peaches and jam; stir until the jam melts. Stir in the catsup, vinegar and tabasco. Transfer to a blender and blend until the peaches are coarsely chopped. Cool and store in the refrigerator until needed.

Rinse the fillets and pat dry. Combine the flour, thyme, salt and pepper in a bowl. Dredge the fillets in flour; shake off excess. Heat the oil and 1 tb butter in a frying pan. Add the pecans and stir until fragrant (1-2 minutes). Set the pecans aside and add the fish to the pan without overlapping. Cook until the fish is crisp and golden on the bottom, about 4 minutes. Turn and cook another 4 minutes until the fish is opaque. Warm the ginger-peach sauce and spoon over the fish, sprinkle with pecans.

Gammon River

Type Mid-sized wilderness whitewater river
Difficulty Intermediate
Distance 106 km
Time 3-4 days
Access By plane to Obukowin Lake or by canoe from Wallace Lake via Siderock Lake and the Obukowin portage.
Egress At the junction of Gammon and Bloodvein rivers.
Topo Maps 52L14, 52M3, 52M5, 52M6
Season May to September

The Gammon River system is an enjoyable blend of lakes and rivers. It is often shallow, sandy and very clear for a shield river. With three lakes and a drop of only 48 metres the current is negligible and the shoreline is frequently low and marshy. The rapids occur where the river crosses a ridge and are usually widely spaced.

The Obukowin portage out of Wallace Lake is commonly used to access the Gammon River. The Bloodvein, Pigeon, Berens and Poplar can also be reached via a series of portages starting at Wallace Lake. There is also a portage directly into

Aikens Lake on the Gammon River via the Wanipigow and Broadleaf rivers, but it is not recommended because of the many beaver dams.

At Wallace Lake there is a provincial campground, boat launch and parking lot. You can either portage or paddle to Siderock Lake. Even though the portage is over a kilometre long, it is very flat, dry and well-marked, whereas the Wanipigow River wanders aimlessly through a swamp before reaching Siderock Lake. From the campground proceed along either shore to the south-

Paul Krilyk starting the "bog ballet."

east corner of the lake. The portage to Siderock Lake is in the centre of the bay.

The portage out of Siderock Lake is about three kilometres east on the north (left) side of the lake. It is difficult to spot, so drift along the shore until you come to an opening in the bushes. There is a good campsite on the east end of the big island where canoeists often camp before tackling the Obukowin portage.

The infamous Obukowin portage crosses a creek and two small lakes in its five kilometre length. The trail is well used and maintained, and even though it goes through a recent burn there is little deadfall. The first obstacle is the creek, which has to be paddled, waded or hiked depending on recent beaver activity. From the creek it is a long march to the first lake. With luck you can paddle down the creek to the lake proper, otherwise it is a muddy walk. Roll up your pants and drag the canoe across 30 metres of floating bog to the base of the ridge at the second bay on the east side of the lake where the

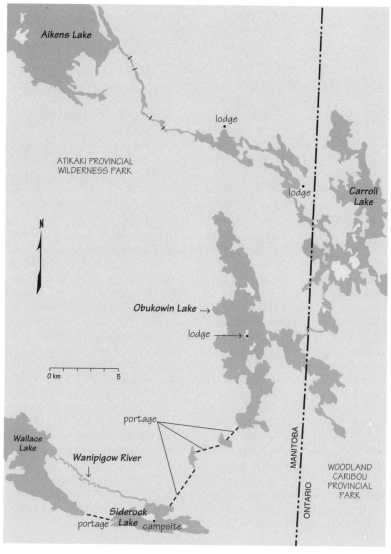

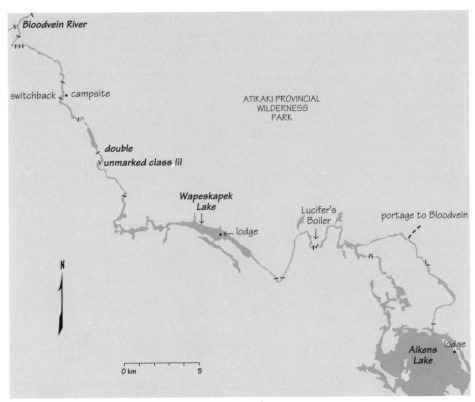

Bloodvein River

switchback •campsite

ATIKAKI PROVINCIAL
WILDERNESS
PARK

double
unmarked class lil

Wapeskapek
Lake

Lucifer's
Boiler

portage to Bloodvein

lodge

N

Aikens   lodge
Lake

0 km   5

portage resumes. This portion of the portage was burned in 1987 so follow the cairns carefully to the second lake. Practise your "bog ballet" as you leap gracefully from log to log dragging your fully loaded canoe across another floating bog. Paddle straight across the lake to the rock point (thank dryness) where the portage continues. This final section crosses several small ridges and intervening wet valleys before the final steep descent to Obukowin.

Obukowin Lake is weedy and the west side has been burned, but there are still many good campsites on the islands and peninsulas. The outlet to Carroll Lake is obscured with wild rice in late summer but the river is usually navigable.

A 1.2 metre-high waterfall marks the Ontario border and the entrance to Woodland Caribou Provincial Park. Another kilometre down the river brings you to Carroll Lake, a large lake with many beautiful islands, bays, channels and straits. Judging from the number of fishing camps the fishing must be exceptionally good in Carroll. After a leisurely four kilometres you reach the Manitoba border and enter the Gammon River, although at this point it is indistinguishable from the lake.

The first rapid on the Gammon, a curving class I, is another three kilometres downstream. There is a picturesque campsite here on river right that is easily missed as the rapid claims all of your attention. After this first rapid the river broadens and you have five kilometres of relaxed paddling before the river again narrows and the first portage is reached, a 60 pacer on river left around a six metre-high waterfall.

Past the waterfall the Gammon is clear and shallow with a sandy bottom, and it is a pleasure to paddle. Only a class II rapid with a portage on river

Author breaking camp. Photo: Gerry Reckseidler.

right followed shortly by a four metre-high waterfall with a 50-pace portage on river left bars the way to Aikens Lake.

Aikens Lake is a large open body of water and should only be crossed when winds are light. Unfortunately, much of the shoreline at the river mouth has been burned in recent years and camping spots are in short supply. Therefore it is best to arrive at Aikens early in the morning when it is usually calm. Crossing Aikens, head for the gap between the two big islands west of the river mouth. There are many shoals in Aikens Lake and not all of them are marked. The gap between the two islands is very shallow and the bow paddler has to keep a sharp eye out for rocks to avoid being grounded. The branch of the Gammon flowing out of the north end of Aikens is usually navigable only during the spring.

There is a fishing lodge on the east side of Aikens Lake where you might find shelter if conditions make crossing the lake risky, but the owners are not known to be charitable toward canoeists.

Leaving Aikens Lake behind, continue down the Gammon. This section of the Gammon to Lucifer's Boiler is very picturesque as the river snakes through narrow, granite-lined passages and several class II-III rapids. At Lucifer's Boiler, which is a five metre-high waterfall, an island dividing the river has an idyllic campsite at the downstream end of the island. A double portage is required on river right, then double back to view the falls.

The low, marshy terrain, for the next 20 kilometres to the other side of Wapeskapek Lake, restricts camping opportunities. The rapids are easy class I or II's so the distance is covered quickly. The east end of Wapeskapek Lake is shallow and weedy and the west end was badly burned in 1983. A fly-in fishing lodge on the biggest island has the best spot for camping. Where the river turns north again, the burn and marsh are left behind.

The first rapid in this section is a class I, followed in two kilometres by an unmarked class III, which is portaged river right. The next rapid is a double with the upper being a waterfall and the lower a class I-II. The portage, on river right, is easily missed as it crosses the base of the peninsula and starts before the rapid is visible or audible. If the first portage is missed there is a second portage, on river left, that goes around the waterfall only.

Continuing down the river the next rapid is best lined, then there is a class III, at the switchback, where the last good campsite before the Bloodvein is located. At the next rapid there is no established portage but luckily it is only a class I. From here it is five kilometres to the final four rapids on the Gammon, clustered together less than a kilometre from the Bloodvein.

At the first of these final rapids, paddle past the obvious portage on river left and take the left channel between the shore and rock outcropping. The placid water here compared with the violent rapid a paddle length on your left suggests something ominous ahead. At the end of the channel there is a small bay with the suspected waterfall at the outlet requiring a lift-over. The next two rapids are falls with the second one appearing to have a runnable gap on river right. I have always been deterred by pieces of broken canoe found at the base of the gap. The final rapid is an easy class I past a sheer face that seems ideal for pictographs. No pictographs are present even though an archaeological site is known to exist at the junction of the rivers.

There is a small campsite on river left at the junction of the Bloodvein, and there is a trapper's cabin about three kilometres downstream. The cabin is suitable for a floatplane pick-up if you are not continuing on the Bloodvein.

Ray's Fish Chowder

The Gammon River always seems to have a plentiful supply of fish in spite of the number of fishing lodges. I learned this tasty method of preparing fresh-caught fish from an old guide.

Servings: 4
1/2 cup onions
2 lg potatoes
1/2 lb side bacon (or bacon bits)
1 lb fresh fish
2 tb butter
1/2 ts pepper
pinch of sugar
1/2 cup skim milk powder
1 ts paprika

At home, chop and dry the onions and potatoes. Crumble the fried bacon and preserve in lard. At camp, scale the fish and cut into 2 inch chunks. Boil the fish until the flesh is opaque and falls off the bones. Remove the bones and skin from the fish chunks. Sauté the bacon in butter or lard. Bring 3 cups of water to boil. Add the deboned fish and remaining ingredients except the milk and paprika. Cover and boil gently 10-15 minutes. Stir in the milk powder and simmer for 5 minutes. Serve garnished with paprika. If desired, bacon bits can be substituted for side bacon.

Jim McKay and Ray Ingalls portaging a beaver dam.

Ray Ingalls in swamp.

Little Saskatchewan River

Type A dam-controlled river flowing through a deep, picturesque valley.
Difficulty Intermediate
Distance 37 km
Time 1-2 days
Access Boat launch in Rivers Provincial Park at Rivers, Manitoba.
Egress At the confluence of Assiniboine River west of Brandon.
Topo Maps 62F16 and 62K1
Season April to May or whenever the dam is releasing water.

From its Lake Audy source, in Manitoba's Riding Mountain National Park, to man-made Lake Wahtopanah at Rivers, Manitoba the Little Saskatchewan winds placidly through a broad river valley. The section above Minnedosa is an enjoyable float especially in the early spring when the river spills its banks and you can canoe across the meanders. At this time of year, waterfowl are migrating and geese, ducks, herons, plovers and sandpipers by their thousands are resting in the calm waters before continuing north. However, each year seems to bring more clearing of the river valley for agriculture thus making it less interesting for canoeing.

The last section of the Little Saskatchewan between Rivers and the Assiniboine River flows through a narrow, undisturbed valley. The river drops 100 metres in 38 kilometres for an astonishing 2.6 metres per kilometre and yet there are no falls, only a steady descent and a reach of class I rapids that is unequalled. There are only two short portages in this section. The current makes it possible to paddle this section in about eight hours, but to appreciate the beauty of it two full days are recommended.

Rapids and sunbathers at the remains of Manitoba's first hydro station.

Rivers Provincial Park with its campground and boat launch is the preferred starting point for this portion of the river. It is also possible to launch canoes at the spillway below the dam or at Kiwanis Park on Hwy. #25.

From the boat launch paddle west across the lake to the second inlet, which leads to the dam and spillway. To avoid being swept over the spillway take-out on river left well above the dam and follow the path to the small bay at the base of the spillway.

Past Hwy. #25 and looking like a scene from a grade B western, the CNR mainline spans the valley on a trestle bridge towering 30 metres over the river. I envision an ancient steam locomotive being pursued by cowboys chugging

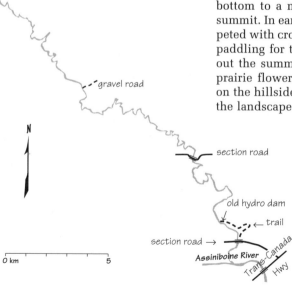

across the bridge. About half a kilometre downstream from the bridge there is an unmarked low-profile weir or dam and the second and final portage. Weirs are well known for their dangerous hydraulics and this one is no exception. It is all that remains of the CPR bridge that crossed the river here prior to 1980. This short portage is on river right and follows a dirt road to a pool below the weir from where the remainder of the rapid can be run.

The next portion of the river consists of almost continuous class I rapids that will put your back ferrying skills to a superb test to avoid the many rocks and tight turns in the river. Watch for the blue heron rookery on river left about two kilometres downstream. After seven kilometres the frequency of the rapids decreases somewhat and allows opportunities to admire the aspen- and oak-covered hills towering up to 30 metres above the river. There are many good campsites in the next 10 kilometres and the hills above the river are well worth hiking and exploring. The valley has remained undisturbed and it showcases a microcosm of Manitoba's ecology ranging from an oak-aspen river bottom to a mixed-grass prairie at the summit. In early spring the hills are carpeted with crocus and the river is worth paddling for this sight alone. Throughout the summer a succession of native prairie flowers can be found blooming on the hillsides, adding their colours to the landscape and attracting a wide va-

Highway bridge made from recycled railway bridge.

riety of birds. As the river here is crossing the Manitoba escarpment the soil is a mixture of sand and gravel. This is certainly preferred for camping to the gumbo often found along prairie rivers.

Where a gravel road comes in from the left the valley widens a little and is more cultivated. A few farms are visible on the hillsides and several fords are passed before arriving at a recycled railway bridge carrying a section road across the river. Fence lines frequently run to the river's edge but I did not find any crossing the river. However, you should watch carefully in this area.

Once past the bridge the valley is more wooded and high hills again border the river. About five kilometres past the bridge the river flows around an island and the rapid here should be scouted as there is an abrupt drop and a standing wave at high water levels. Located another kilometre downstream is the remains of Manitoba's first hydroelectric generating station. Built in 1900, the plant supplied electricity to Brandon until 1924. Today, all that remains are the concrete piers and a long

class I rapid that requires several back ferries to navigate between the rocks.

Located around the bend from the piers is the remnants of Glen Orky downhill ski resort. Some of the old runs are still visible twisting down the steep hills. These steep hills attracted more than downhill skiers: They were used as buffalo jumps by the early native cultures who would stampede the buffalo over the precipice, causing them to fall to their death. Less than a kilometre away is the Stott Site, an archaeology dig that unearthed evidence of bison hunting here 5,000 years ago.

To reach the Assiniboine River there are a few more tight bends where the river tries to push you against the steep outside bank in a last effort to upset your canoe, as well as two class I rapids. After the rush of the Little Saskatchewan, the placid pace of the wide Assiniboine is an abrupt change. It's only another two kilometres, down the Assiniboine, to the Trans-Canada Highway with the take-out on river right under the first bridge.

Tunisian Vegetable Stew

This is another tasty vegetarian meal. Because of the cans and cheese this meal is best suited for an overnight trip on an easy river like the Little Saskatchewan River where there are no portages.

Servings: 4
1-1/2 cups onions
3 cups cabbage
1 lg green pepper
2 tb olive oil
1 dash salt
2 ts coriander
1/2 ts turmeric
1/4 ts cinnamon
1/8 ts cayenne
3 cups tomatoes
1-1/2 cups canned chick-peas
1/2 cup raisins
1 tb lemon juice
1/2 cup feta

Slice the onions, cabbage and pepper very thin. In a large skillet sauté the onions in olive oil for 5 minutes. Add the cabbage and sprinkle with salt. Sauté for 5 minutes, stirring occasionally. Add the pepper and spices and sauté for a minute. Stir in the tomatoes, chick-peas and raisins and simmer, covered, for 15 minutes until the vegetables are tender. Add the lemon juice. Serve over rice or couscous and top with the feta.

Manigotagan River

Type Mid-sized wilderness river with many waterfalls and some cottage development.
Difficulty Intermediate
Distance 134 km
Time 4-7 days
Access Bridge on Hwy. #314 near Long Lake. Parking and boat launch on southeast side.
Egress Bridge on Hwy. #304 at Manigotagan. Parking on northeast side.
Topo Maps 52L11, 52L13, 52L14, 52M4, 62P1
Other Maps *Bucky's RiverRunner Guide*, Berard's Oiseau-Manigotagan Routes
Season May to September

The Manigotagan River is a favourite of Manitoba canoeists because it usually has ample flow throughout the summer, many rapids of all levels of difficulty, road access and egress, and it flows through a wilderness area. A massive fire in 1983 burned much of the drainage basin of this stream between Long Lake and the Ontario border. The area is regrowing slowly but the fire scars are still highly visible along the river. Another fire in 1989 marred the 30 last kilometres of the river.

The Manigotagan undoubtedly was used in pre-contact times but only archaeological records remain. In historic times the river was used to bring supplies to the Tene and Wadhope gold mines near Long Lake. It can be accessed via the Moose River, Hwy. #314, Long Lake or Quesnel Lake. The latter is a common starting point because Caribou Lake Lodge offers an excellent campground on the lake and it is an easy three-day trip back to Hwy. #304. The owners of Caribou Lake Lodge can arrange car shuttles so your vehicle will be waiting for you when you arrive. The Moose River access is not recommended because the forest fire in 1983 obliterated the portage into Lily Lake and it has not been reopened. The watercourse shown on the topographical map exists only in the cartographer's imagination.

From Hwy. #314 a road, 200 metres south of the bridge, leads to the river and a boat launch. Depending on the water levels, it is possible to canoe through one of the culverts rather than portaging across the road. An abandoned wayside park is located on the north side of the bridge but there is no river access.

From the road it is 1.5 kilometres to the first rapids. This is a set of three rapids separated by about 100 metres

Sharon Macdonald and Dennis Leneveu at Charles Falls.

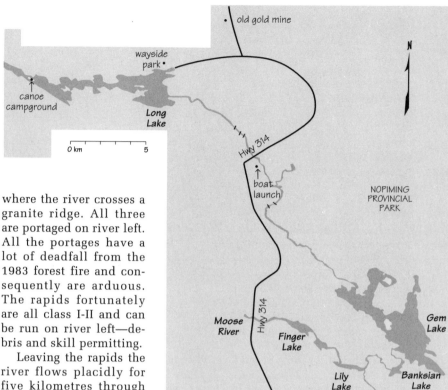

where the river crosses a granite ridge. All three are portaged on river left. All the portages have a lot of deadfall from the 1983 forest fire and consequently are arduous. The rapids fortunately are all class I-II and can be run on river left—debris and skill permitting.

Leaving the rapids the river flows placidly for five kilometres through low, swampy country to Long Lake. Long Lake has been developed with a summer cottage subdivision but there are two designated canoe campgrounds on the lake.

Departing Long Lake the river makes a sharp left revealing a hidden ledge with a one metre drop and a very narrow chute. The portage is on river left and starts before the ledge is visible. Three more waterfalls with the obligatory portages are encountered before reaching Manigotagan Lake. From Long Lake to Caribou Landing on Quesnel Lake it is typical Shield country. The short stretch between Long and Manigotagan is seldom used and sightings of moose and caribou are not unusual. Manigotagan and Quesnel lakes are popular fishing spots and attract many motorboats on weekends.

At Manigotagan Lake follow the right shore to find the entrance to Quesnel

Lake. There is an old trapper's cabin on the right as you enter Quesnel Lake. The lake was named after Bidou Quesnel, an early settler in the area.

The largest island on Quesnel has a canoe campground and firepit but a recent fire makes this an unappealing site. Caribou Lake Lodge on the north side of the lake is a private campground with tent sites, cabins and a store. The present owners always have the welcome mat out for canoeists. This is a friendly place to rest up and gather information and supplies before continuing your journey. It is 76 kilometres to Hwy. #304, which makes it an easy three-day trip. This part of the Manigotagan with its many exhilarating rapids is an excellent introduction to wilderness river canoeing and is heavily

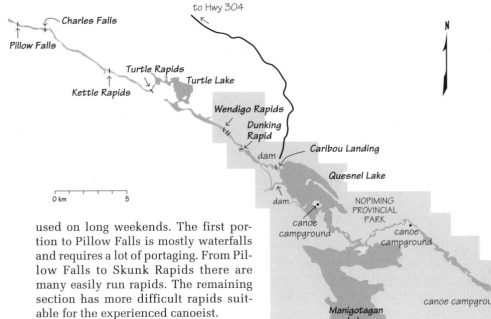

used on long weekends. The first portion to Pillow Falls is mostly waterfalls and requires a lot of portaging. From Pillow Falls to Skunk Rapids there are many easily run rapids. The remaining section has more difficult rapids suitable for the experienced canoeist.

Leaving Quesnel Lake portage on river right past a crushed rock dam. This dam was originally built during the gold rush days to regulate water levels. One-half kilometre farther there is a waterfall where the river splits into five channels as it thunders over the rocks.

In another 1.5 kilometres there is a deceptive rapid known affectionately as Dunking Rapid. It is a class III that should be runnable on river right but in spite of many attempts I have never succeeded. The current forces you into the keeper at the base of the ledge where your canoe fills with water and slowly sinks while you get washed out through the rest of the rapid. The water is deep and the rapid is short, so it is worth a try in warm weather. For those readers who prefer to remain dry there is a portage on river left.

An easy class I in the next kilometre is followed by a class IV known as Wendigo Rapids. This is the longest portage on the Manigotagan so it will give you an opportunity to dry out as you tote your gear across this long, flat portage.

Wendigo Rapids is on the western edge of Nopiming Provincial Park.

Abitibi-Price has a logging permit along the rest of the river and may build bridges to access timber on the south side of the river. Watch for signs of clear-cutting and be especially careful near any sign of construction.

From Wendigo Rapids it is seven kilometres across marshy Turtle Lake to Turtle Rapids, portaged on river right. It is another 2.5 kilometres to Kettle Rapids, the site of a proposed bridge. There is a short, steep portage around rapid. A deadhead at the end makes this rapid a risky run.

The campsite at six metre-high Charles Falls, conveniently situated 20 kilometres from Caribou Landing, is one of the nicest on the river. There are very few campsites in the next 10 kilometres and most are suitable for only one tent.

The 4.5 metre-high Pillow Falls, about 1.5 kilometres after Charles, is the last waterfall before a long series of exciting class I and II rapids. A steep portage on river right goes around this impressive waterfall.

There are 10 class I rapids in the next 22 kilometres culminating in the class II

Skunk Rapids. Unfortunately, this is a low, marshy area and the scenery is rather monotonous. A large fire in 1989 burned the area between Hwy. #304 and Skunk Rapids making the scenery even more unappealing.

Watch for the remains of "The Alligator" in the willow thickets on river left between the third and fourth rapids after Pillow Falls. Legend has it that this boat carried an ore crusher and was on its way to the gold mines near Long Lake when the crew abandoned it after the cook quit. It is claimed that the contraption winched itself past rapids using anchors set into the bedrock. This would have been a fascinating spectacle to watch at the many waterfalls. Considering the damage to my canoe, from portage take-outs and put-ins, I suspect that "The Alligator" sunk from all the holes in the hull.

Skunk Rapids is the first of the final series of rapids. The rapids in this section are more challenging and most of them are runnable. However, scouting is mandatory for all of this section.

The portage at the class II Skunk Rapids is on river left. There is a small campsite at the lower end of the portage.

From Skunk Rapids it is less than a kilometre to Big Eddy Rapids, perhaps the best known and most photographed rapid on the Manigotagan. Big Eddy is a double set with the upper a difficult class III where the river drops over two ledges separated by about six metres. The 100-pace portage on river left leads to the big circular eddy between the two rapids. From the eddy you must cross the outwash of the upper rapid without being pushed into the rock wall on your left, then run the lower class I rapid. Fortunately, there is a good campsite here to give you lots of time to plan your manoeuvres or build up enough courage to run the upper set.

At Cascade Rapids, another 1.5 kilometres, there is a 1.5 metre-high waterfall in the middle of what would otherwise be a demanding class II rapid. There are portages on both sides of the river. The portage on river left is the longer and more difficult but you can put-in below the falls and run the remainder. The one on river right goes around the entire rapid.

Leaving Cascade, it is a two kilometre paddle to the class II Engineer Rapids. The ledge on river right at the end of Engineer looks straightforward but can be

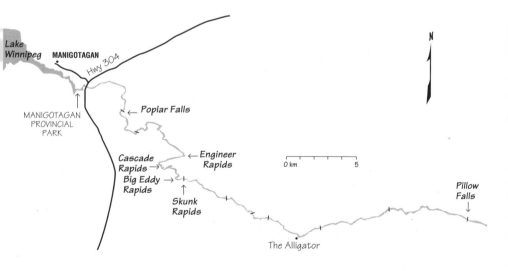

Author and Dennis Leneveu at Big Eddy Rapids.

Author and Sharon Macdonald at remains of "The Alligator."

very dangerous because of the keeper at the end of the ledge. If you attempt this run, have a rescue boat downstream and a throw rope on the rock in the centre. The portage on river left is much safer.

A long, narrow island straddles the river two kilometres below Engineer. There is a good, but heavily used, campsite on the island and a short portage across the island. The river drops over a two metre-high waterfall on either side of the island.

A kilometre-and-a-half down river are two class I-II rapids. They are very rocky and require precise manoeuvring at flows between 10 and 15 cubic ft./sec (cfs). Below 10 cfs lining is usually necessary and above 15 cfs most of the rocks are deep enough that it is an easy, if rough, rapid to run. Both rapids have a portage on river right.

The last portage is a wet, 280 paces on river right at the 4.5 metre-high Poplar Falls. It is approximately 4.5 kilometres past marshy shoreline to Hwy. #304. The take-out is on river right about 30 metres before the bridge over Wood Falls.

Pasta Diablo

Pasta is always a favourite meal on canoe trips. I was introduced to this hot and spicy variation on the Manigotagan River after several unsuccessful attempts at running Big Eddy Rapids.

Servings: 4
4 tb New Mexican red chillies
1/2 cup sun-dried tomatoes
1 cup black olives
1/2 cup basil
2 tb lemon juice
2 ts black pepper
1 lb Penne pasta
1/2 cup Italian parsley
3/4 lb parmesan cheese
1 tb grated lemon peel
3 garlic cloves
1/2 cup olive oil

Crush the chillies, dice the tomatoes, pit the olives, chop the basil and parsley, and grate the cheese. Combine all the ingredients except the cheese and pasta and let sit for a few hours to blend flavours. Cook the pasta in 4 quarts of water until tender but firm. Drain. Toss the pasta with the sauce and cheese and serve.

Ochre River

Type Small whitewater river
Difficulty Expert
Distance 25 km
Time 1 day
Access Proceed south on Hwy. #582 from the town of Ochre River. Take the first right after the second bridge. Turn right after 1.6 km and follow this road to the Riding Mountain National Park border. Portage 600 metres to the river along the fire road.
Egress Bridge on Hwy. #582.
Topo Maps 62J13, 62O4
Season April to May

The Ochre River flows from the heights of Riding Mountain National Park down the steep north face and into Dauphin. Lake. There is no canoe access to the upper reaches of the river because it is inside the park. Starting at the park boundary, where a fire road gives access to the river, the Ochre River has a gradient of five m/km (26 ft./mi.) for the first 10 kilometres and has a maximum width of seven metres. Fortunately, there are no waterfalls, so the river is an exciting and challenging run for experienced canoeists when the water is high. Because of the small catchment basin and the steep gradient, most of the year there is insufficient water to paddle this delightful river. The only times to canoe it are during spring runoff or after a heavy summer storm.

For the first kilometre from the park border, virtually continuous rapids in this narrow, boulder-strewn river require your constant attention and all your skills. This is followed by an area of gravel bars and sweepers where the river pauses briefly before continuing its precipitous descent. Next there is a narrow, sheer-walled, black shale canyon delicately papered with bright green mosses that trickle continuously.

Five kilometres from the start is Scane Crossing, a ford and picnic site built by the Turtle River Conservation District. Don't be surprised if a truck or tractor splashes across the shallows in front of your canoe. Pause here to recover from the rapids or better yet, return to run them again.

Leaving Scane Crossing, the river enters a short, narrow, twisting canyon. The rapids continue, but with fewer canoe-crunching rocks to avoid, the paddling is less stressful. Slowly the height of the banks decrease until Hwy. #582 is reached. This is an ideal spot to end the trip or return to the start for yet another run. From here to Hwy. #5 the river is very narrow, sluggish and has slick clay banks.

Overlook at put-in.

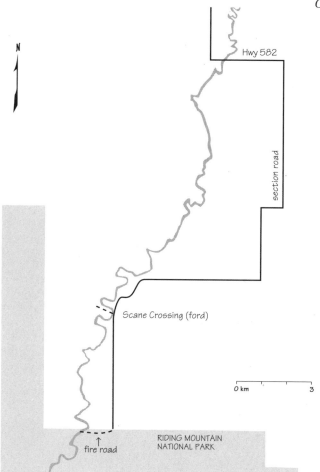

N

Hwy 582

section road

Scane Crossing (ford)

0 km   3

fire road

RIDING MOUNTAIN
NATIONAL PARK

Hot Mint Chocolate

The Ochre River can only be run in the early spring when the water is high
and cold. The weather is often cold at this time and it's a certainty that you
will get wet running the rapids in this boisterous river. A cup of hot choco-
late at lunch warms you and restores your sugar levels.
   Servings: 8
   2 tb cocoa powder
   5 tb powdered milk
   2 tb mint tea powder
   7 tb brown sugar
Mix the ingredients and store in a waterproof plastic bag. At camp, add 2
tb of the mixture to 1 cup of steaming hot water and stir until dissolved.

Pembina River

Type Small pastoral flatwater river. Excellent bird watching in spring.
Difficulty Beginner
Distance 34 km
Time 1-2 days
Access Conner's Bridge 20 km south of the town of Manitou.
Egress Bridge on Hwy. #201, five km east of Windygates. Park on the northeast corner.
Topo Maps 62G1 and 62G2
Season March to April

Meandering across southwestern Manitoba from its origins in the Turtle Mountains to La Riviere, the Pembina River flows through a broad valley of mixed farms. It is a small river bordered with heavy brush. South of La Riviere the valley narrows as the river crosses the Manitoba escarpment before finally flowing into North Dakota near Windygates. There are no rapids but the brisk current and occasional fallen tree, called sweepers, or the undercut bank can cause problems for the inattentive.

Near Hwy. #31 several Wildlife Management Areas bordering on the river provide wildlife habitat for deer and outstanding viewing opportunities for canoeists. In the spring the constricted valley at Hwy. #201 concentrates migrating birds. Over 2,000 red-tailed hawks have been observed here on a single day!

Downstream of La Riviere there are seven bridges crossing the river and any one of them can be used for access or egress. Rather than one long trip, a series of day trips can be made using the bridges.

Scenery along the Pembina.

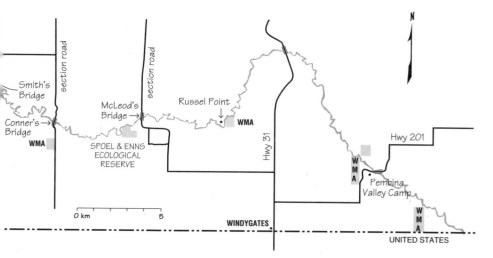

Upstream of Conner's Bridge the riverbank is muddy and livestock frequent the river's edge. The most scenic part of the river is from Conner's Bridge to Holo Crossing (Hwy. #201). Although I have never encountered any barbed wire fences crossing the river, it would be prudent to watch for and avoid any fences.

At Conner's Bridge the banks subside; the river widens and braids over a series of shale bars. The low banks and open country give an impressive view of this wide valley. The concrete abutments are all that remain of Conner's Bridge. Three large culverts now carry the river underneath the road. These culverts replace a single smaller culvert that along with the road was washed out in the heavy summer rains of 1993.

Past Conner's Bridge, the high, wooded banks again close in on the river, but it is still shallow and there are many gravel bars and some sweepers. Occasionally, abandoned buildings are visible but the predominant feature is heavily wooded hillsides much as it must have been before European settlers arrived. Mud banks and a low, marshy area appear briefly when rounding a large peninsula that borders the Spoel and Enns Ecological Reserve, protecting a mixed-grass prairie. The shallows and gravel bars return by the time you reach McLeod's Bridge. A good take-out with ample parking can be found on the northeast side of the bridge. Running the culverts at McLeod's Bridge is hazardous because the downstream end of the culverts have been eroded, creating a large standing wave. The culverts are scheduled to be replaced in the near future.

From McLeod's Bridge to Hwy. #31 the banks are lower and more of the valley is visible. This area is mostly used for grazing but some parts are cropped, especially on the south side of the river. Past Russel Point the Pembina Valley Wildlife Management Area borders the river and there are fewer signs of agricultural usage and more wildlife.

The final section of the Pembina River from Hwy. #31 to Holo Crossing is arguably the most scenic on the river. Averaging about two kilometres wide and 120 metres deep, the valley slopes are covered with elm, green ash, Manitoba maple, basswood, birch and the ever present aspen. These trees provide a rich habitat for wildlife. Two more Wildlife Management Areas along this stretch preserve and protect the indigenous wildlife of the valley. Pembina Valley Camp, at the sum-

Scenery along the Pembina cliffs.

mit on the west side at Holo Crossing, has constructed a network of hiking trails skirting the valley summit and descending to the river. Spend a strenuous afternoon hiking the trails or quietly watching the abundant bird life from one of the observation towers.

Instead of utilizing a car shuttle, plan to ride your bike back to the starting point, but be prepared for a steep climb out of the valley. A delicious end to any canoe trip would be a meal in Maida, which is known for its restaurant, and is just across the border from Windygates.

Hummus

Hummus is a common dish from the Middle East. It is light, quick and nutritious, and therefore ideal for canoeing. My middle son discovered it and passed the menu on to me. Powdered hummus can also be purchased for use on long trips when fresh hummus is not available. It is delicious for lunches, which is the main meal on the Pembina River.

Servings: 4
2 cans chick-peas
6 tb tahini (sesame seed paste)
3 cloves garlic
1/3 cup lemon juice
salt and pepper to taste
2 tb olive oil
dash paprika
1/4 cup parsley

Combine all the ingredients, except olive oil, paprika and parsley, in a blender adding 1/8 of the reserved liquid. Blend to a smooth creamy paste. It should be the creamy consistency of mashed potatoes. Thin with chick-pea liquid. Add lemon juice or salt to taste. Package in a waterproof container. At lunch, garnish with olive oil, paprika and parsley. Serve as dip for pita bread and raw vegetables.

Pigeon River

Type Mid-sized wilderness whitewater river
Difficulty Intermediate
Distance 153 km
Time 5-9 days
Access By plane to Shinning Falls on Family Lake.
Egress By plane from the mouth of the river or paddle to Berens River.
Topo Maps 52M13, 62P16, 63A1, 63A2
Other Maps Berard's Little Grand Rapids Routes
Season May to September

The Pigeon is Manitoba's finest whitewater river. With an assured flow from Family Lake, the paddling is excellent all summer. Canoeing the small, narrow channels of the Pigeon gives you an intimate feeling for this river. Unlike the Berens, only a few miles north, most of the rapids on the Pigeon are runnable by experienced canoeists. There is little indication river was much used by early traders and explorers. They preferred the Berens because of its generally shorter portages.

From Shinning Falls, the highest waterfall on the east side of Lake Winnipeg, to Vicker's Lake there are five sets of rapids. The most difficult are between Am-

Jeannine Macaulay and Gerry Reckseidler enjoying an unnamed rapid on the Pigeon.

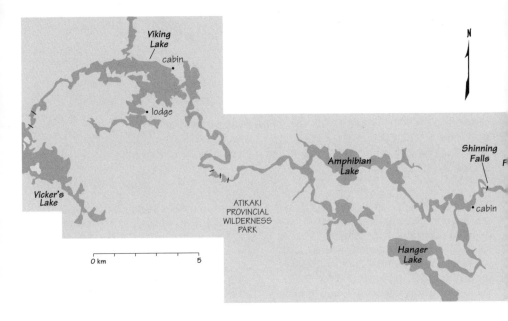

phibian and Vicker's lakes, with two class III rapids in close proximity, but this is mostly low, swampy country. Amphibian and Viking lakes are both very weedy. Because the river is clear with a sandy bottom, it is likely a good pickerel river. There is very little evidence of recent forest fires, making this a beautiful area to paddle and camp in.

Rock-infested Vicker's Lake has a wealth of campsites on the islands at the west end of the lake. With its selection of bays and islets, this is an enticing lake to spend a day exploring or losing fishing tackle to the many voracious rocks lurking just below the surface.

There are four exits from Vicker's Lake and water levels dictate which should be used. To the north there is a class I in a very narrow channel and the high rock on both sides makes portaging difficult. The middle two exits are high water channels only. A 100 pace portage on river left is required on the southern passage past the class III-IV rapid.

Whitewater rafting trips use the 40 kilometre section between Vicker's and Round lakes. Over 30 rapids are found here, including the renowned "canyon," making this the most attractive section of the Pigeon River for whitewater enthusiasts.

At the big island about 10 kilometres past Vicker's Lake the left channel has three class VI waterfalls to portage. In the right channel, the rapids are in parallel rather than series and only one or two portages are required, depending on your skill and route chosen. The three ledges of the centre passage are often the easiest route. On the left side there is a particularly attractive campsite but a difficult rapid. Both channels lead to a waterfall. The last rapid on the right channel is a ledge followed by a waterfall requiring a portage on river left of 100 paces.

In the next 12 kilometres there are many rapids and waterfalls where the river is squeezed through narrow gorges. Excellent campsites and short portages can be found at almost all the rapids. With all the portaging and scouting necessary it is slow travelling, so plan to spend an extra day or two playing in the rapids.

Following this slow section, the river runs straight northwest for nine kilometres. The first rapid encountered is "the

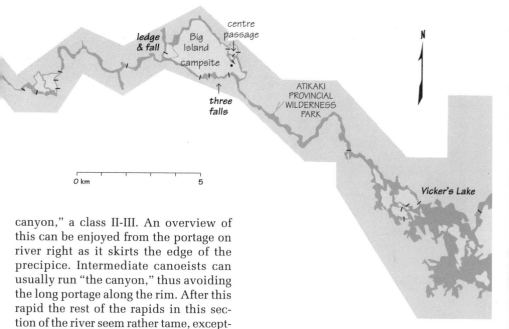

canyon," a class II-III. An overview of this can be enjoyed from the portage on river right as it skirts the edge of the precipice. Intermediate canoeists can usually run "the canyon," thus avoiding the long portage along the rim. After this rapid the rest of the rapids in this section of the river seem rather tame, excepting a class III ledge.

At the next large island both channels require two portages around waterfalls, but the falls on the left channel are magnificent. They are known locally as Island Falls. Judging from the campsites it is a popular place to stop.

Between Island Falls and Round Lake the rapids are all class III or better. The second last one is called Round-about. One group, in attempting to run this rapid, capsized and their canoe was caught in the eddy and went around several times before finally being washed out.

Past Round Lake the rapids are again mostly class III or better. At the island, two kilometres downstream of Round Lake there is an almost runnable class III in the left channel and two waterfalls in the right channel.

About seven kilometres past Round Lake a peninsula juts into the river. There is a class III rapid in the left channel and the portage is at the end of the blind bay on the right. A good campsite exists on the tip of the peninsula with an excellent trail beside the rapid that is designed for scouting or fishing.

Two unmarked class I's are run before reaching the island where the river turns west. Use the left channel as the right is only passable at high water. The marked rapid, on the left, is a class I-II.

Turning west, the river slows its headlong rush to Lake Winnipeg and the rapids are less frequent. The next one is a series of four ledges that can be portaged or lined on river right. At the end there is a lovely campsite, the best before Sturgeon Falls.

At Poplar Falls use the left channel to avoid the class IV rapid in the main channel. The left channel can be run or lined depending on water levels. This is the last decent campsite before Sturgeon Falls about 22 kilometres farther on.

Leaving Poplar Falls, the land becomes flat and swampy and the current slows to a sedate pace. Not surprisingly the whitewater rafter's camp soon comes into view. In the Windigo Lake area it is reminiscent of walking across a tall-grass prairie. The river is a watery passage through a sea of grass surrounded by a distant ring of black spruce barely visible on the horizon. A solitary rock in this watery wilder-

Gord and Carol Kristjansson at Grant Falls.

Kayaker at three falls.

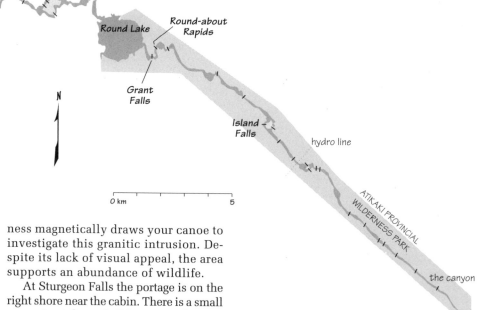

ness magnetically draws your canoe to investigate this granitic intrusion. Despite its lack of visual appeal, the area supports an abundance of wildlife.

At Sturgeon Falls the portage is on the right shore near the cabin. There is a small campsite at the end of the portage but it is heavily used and abused. Judging by the amount of fishing tackle abandoned here the fishing must be superb. The channel on the left side of the island starts with a class I rapid followed by a massive waterfall on both sides of a small island. It is the leading candidate for the most spectacu-lar waterfall in Manitoba. A third unmapped channel exists on the left side of the river but it is passable only at high water levels.

Beyond Sturgeon Falls the land changes again to clay banks and a heavily wooded shoreline. These features keep camping opportunities to a minimum. The bridges shown on the topographical map and built as part of a logging operation have been removed, and the roads are overgrown and are slowly returning to nature.

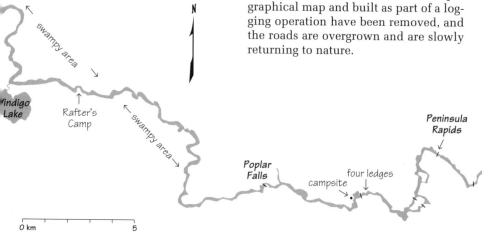

The Chickma II, a former Lake Winnipeg freight boat noted on some maps as being situated at the final rapid, has since been moved to the Selkirk Marine Museum where it has been refurbished and put on display. The museum has a hands-on display of many historic boats from the early days of water transport in Manitoba and is well worth a visit.

While moored on the Pigeon, the Chickma II was used as a bunkhouse for the employees of loggers who cut pulpwood for the Abitibi-Price paper mill at Pine Falls. The main camp of the Channel Area Loggers was located immediately downstream and is easily found by looking for all the discarded machinery on the left shore. Many people choose to end a Pigeon River trip here as it has good access for float planes and it has interesting artifacts to explore while waiting.

It is an additional seven kilometres to Lake Winnipeg. At the mouth two long sand points converge to form a narrow opening into the lake. Sand beaches on the lake side provide a pleasant campsite and the protected bay on the land side has guaranteed pickerel fishing. There are few campsites along the swampy shore of Lake Winnipeg north of the river mouth other than the large, level site at Flathead Point some nine kilometres north across Pigeon Bay. The town of Berens River is another six kilometres beyond Flathead Point. Here you can arrange to ship your canoe home via Waterways or Clarkson Transport and fly to Winnipeg on a scheduled airline.

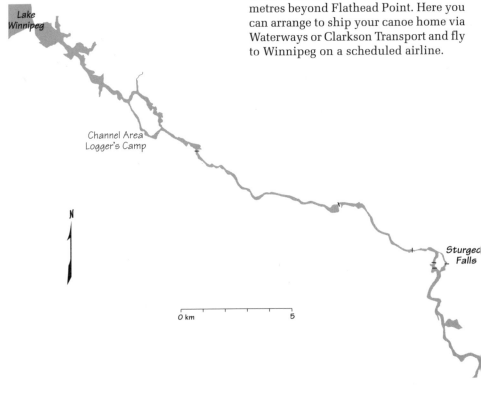

Cajun Pickerel

The turbulent waters of the Pigeon are an ideal habitat for pickerel and every rapid has a few succulent fish waiting to attack your lure. This spicy recipe gives pickerel a distinctive taste. Make the spice mix at home and carry in a zip-lock bag.

Servings: 4
6 tb butter
1 tb cajun spice
2 lb fillets
2 lemons, cut into wedges

Melt the butter in a cast-iron or heavy-bottomed frying pan over medium-high heat. Add the cajun spice and heat thoroughly. Place the fillets in a pan. Squeeze the juice of 1 lemon into the pan. Cook the fish for about 5 minutes on each side. Serve with the remaining lemon wedges and pan drippings.

Cajun Spice
1 tb paprika
1 ts salt
1 ts onion powder
1 ts cayenne powder
1 ts garlic powder
1 ts crushed chillies
1 ts ginger powder
3/4 ts white pepper
3/4 ts black pepper
1/2 ts thyme
1/2 ts oregano

Mix all the ingredients together in a small bowl. Store in an airtight container.

Pinawa Channel

Type Small flatwater river
Difficulty Beginner
Distance 11 km to Hwy. #313
Time 1 day
Access East end of Hwy. #211.
Egress Old Pinawa Dam Provincial Park on Hwy. #520, seven km north of Pinawa or Hwy. #313.
Topo Maps 52L4 and 52L5
Season May to September

In its short 11 kilometre length the Pinawa Channel showcases all the features of Manitoba's Precambrian Shield country in an easily accessible manner. The channel is located 100 kilometres east of Winnipeg at the end of Hwy. #211 near the town of Pinawa on the border of Whiteshell Provincial Park.

The Pinawa Channel was originally used by voyageurs when spring floods made the Seven Sisters section of the Winnipeg River impassable. In 1902 the channel was deepened and straightened to provide a reliable water supply to the hydroelectric plant that was constructed at Pinawa Falls. The plant was decommissioned in 1951 and a rock fill dam was constructed across the mouth of the Pinawa Channel. Today this control dam leaks a steady flow of water and the channel is open all summer.

From the end of Hwy. #211 take the trail north (left) to the rock dam. Scramble down the steep rock face on the far side of the dam and launch your canoe at the base. Noise is effectively screened out by the high canyon walls and except for occasional glimpses of the neighbouring golf course you could be anywhere in Manitoba's wild and rugged Shield country. The narrow, steep-walled, rocky shoreline is studded with startlingly white birch and light green tamarack. In the spring marsh marigolds line the shore.

The extensive blasting that occurred during construction has resulted in many large boulders in the channel, which requires the constant attention of the bow paddler for the first two kilometres. At 2.5 kilometres an island divides the river. On river right a narrow class I rapid rushes beneath a leafy arch. There is no room for a back ferry here, so trusting the rocks are well buried, charge bow first into the standing waves and splash through.

After the rapid the current slows and an additional kilometre brings you to a large swamp that is teeming with birds.

Scenic Pinawa Channel.
Photo: Gerry Reckseidler.

Red-winged and yellow-headed black-birds engage in territorial disputes while Canada geese cruise the shore and black terns wheel overhead.

On the far side of the swamp a narrow finger of land extends across the channel, necessitating a lift-over to avoid the shallow ledges on river right. Located just past the portage is the final class I rapid offering three paths of equal difficulty to choose from.

Leaving the rapid you twist through a short, rocky section and then one kilome-tre of marsh before arriving at the Old Pinawa Dam Provincial Park. The take-out is on river left where the river forms a natural water slide as it sheets down a smooth rock face into a deep hole.

Stop for a swim and a picnic at the park and explore the old hydro site. Reminiscent of Roman ruins, the remains of the old dam and powerhouse rise above the now vanished lake.

The river dropped 12 metres here—the rapids must have been a spectacular sight before the dam was constructed. Walk along the dried-up riverbed and imagine how the river would have looked to voyageurs portaging their canoes past the rapids.

You can finish the trip here or continue another eight kilometres downstream to Hwy. #313. There is no established portage around the old dam. The best route is on river right where several short lift-overs will lead you to the Lee River, as the Pinawa Channel is called downstream of the Pinawa Dam.

The MacArthur Dam on the Winnipeg River, completed in 1951, drowned the remaining rapids on the Lee River and made obsolete the Pinawa Dam. The Lee River is now a wide, slow-moving body of water bordered by farms and summer cottages with a considerable number of powerboats using the river. Turn right after going under the bridge at Hwy. #313 to reach the take-out at the wayside park.

N

Hwy 313

•wayside park

OLD PINAWA DAM
PROVINCIAL PARK

0 km   3

dam

Hwy 211   Hind Island   *Winnipeg River*

Old hydro plant.

Soupe Aux Quatorze Affaires

This original French Canadian pea soup recipe has been handed down from the voyageurs and comes from Louise, a true French Canadian and a great cook. Make up a batch and serve this historic recipe on the Pinawa Channel, an historic route.

Servings: 8
1 lb salt pork
1 tb dry mustard
1 lb dried peas
8 cups cold water
1 lg onion
1/2 ts savoury
1/4 ts mint
1/8 ts thyme
1 garlic clove
1/4 cup parsley
1 tb coarse salt
1 tb butter

Rub the pork with the dry mustard. Cover and refrigerate overnight. Sort and wash the peas. Soak in water for 12 hours.

Add the pork, onion, savoury, mint, thyme, garlic and parsley to the peas. Bring to a boil and simmer 3-4 hours until the peas are tender and the soup looks creamy. Add salt and butter. Serve hot and freeze the leftovers to take canoeing.

Poplar River

Type Large wilderness river with several big lakes
Difficulty Intermediate
Distance 226 km
Time 5-8 days
Access By plane to Sparrowhawk Lake.
Egress By plane from Poplar River Indian Reserve.
Topo Maps 53D5, 53D6, 53D12, 63A9, 63A10, 63A14, 63A15, 63A16, 63H3
Season May to September

The Poplar is the most northerly of the canoeable rivers flowing into Lake Winnipeg. It is rarely canoed, especially the upper reaches. There are several large lakes where a canoeist could be windbound, waterfalls outnumber rapids, there are kilometres of flatwater paddling—often through marshy areas, and there are more fishing lodges than other rivers in Manitoba. In spite of the remoteness the Poplar is not a pristine river. Besides the many fly-in fishing lodges, the river appears to be heavily used by native peoples for hunting, fishing and harvesting wild rice. Evidence of these activities is common along the river. A benefit of all this activity is that the portages are generally easily found and well travelled. Forest fires have extensively scarred the shoreline in many places but this, at least, is a natural phenomena.

The first 40 kilometres, from Sparrowhawk Lake to Kaneekeetawanakeecheewonk Lake, consists of predominantly long, slender lakes separated by rapids ranging from easy class I's to unrunnable waterfalls. These lakes with their myriad islands, headlands and jutting peninsulas are a bow paddler's delight and a navigator's nightmare.

Exiting Sparrowhawk Lake watch for the pictograph on river right just before the first rapid. In spite of the numerous hash lines shown on the topographical map this rapid can be run with only a short portage at the top. The next rapid is a class II-III with a portage on river right. It is a long rapid that drops four metres over a series of three ledges followed by a rock garden. At the third rapid in this section a vertical rock face obliges the river to make an abrupt left turn, obscuring all the rapid beyond the

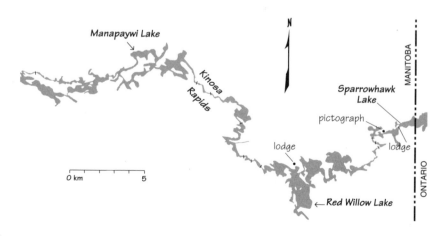

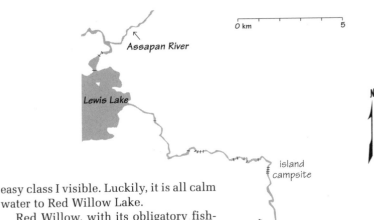

Assapan River

Lewis Lake

N

0 km   5

island
campsite

swampy

Kaneekeetawanakeecheewonk
Lake

← lodge

burn

Manapaywi Lake

easy class I visible. Luckily, it is all calm water to Red Willow Lake.

Red Willow, with its obligatory fishing lodge, is soon crossed and the class III rapid guarding the river entrance portaged. The next rapid has two or more channels, depending on flow, but the left side is the main channel. This is followed by two easy rapids, leading to Kinosa Rapids, a two kilometre stretch containing four rapids with small campsites at the first and last. The Kinosa Rapids are narrow, rocky and usually lack satisfactory flow to be run.

Crossing Manapaywi Lake with its contorted channels and islands requires careful map reading. However, it is a small lake with many enjoyable sites to stretch your limbs so going astray is not a serious problem. Assuming the north exit from the lake is used, two confined waterfalls must be portaged. They are separated by a short canyon of quiet water. Have your cameras handy here.

Leaving the last waterfall, the river widens and the left shore shows signs of a recent burn. Past yet another fishing lodge, the river swings north and a class V rapid must be portaged. The portage is located on river left in the bay before the rapid. The river flows over three ledges, making this a very scenic spot. The portage goes past all three ledges, on a well-used trail.

The rapid denotes the start of a 16 kilometre-long swampy segment of the river. There are a few easy rapids but even these rocky ledges offer no camping opportunities. Not until the river curves west and re-enters forested coun-

try do camping sites recur. The first camping opportunity is at the island where the river curves west. However, it must be a popular spot judging from the amount of garbage on the island. Two unmarked class II-III rapids can be found at the northern tip of the island and lead to the marked class III. This nasty ledge is portaged on the right so using the right channel past the island avoids having to do a quick ferry to safely reach the portage.

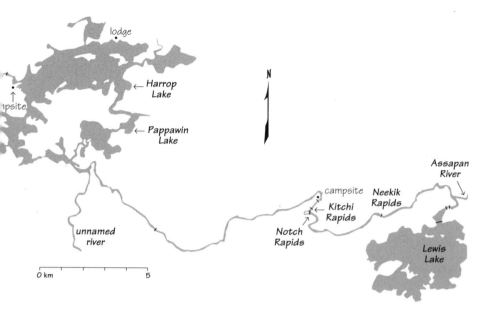

The next two rapids are class I+, followed by a class II at the next island. The left side of the island is shallow and the right narrow, both poor choices as a class III lurks around the corner. The portage here is on river left with a sneak route past the rapid also on the left if you can avoid becoming entangled in the overhanging shrubbery.

The next three rapids are class I-II but often suffer from dearth of water. There is a good portage at the last of this set, but it seems to be much longer than necessary or perhaps I prefer paddling to carrying and cut it short.

The final two rapids in this section are class II-III. At the first rapid, no obvious portage exists but logically it should be on the right. However, the last half can be run so only a short bush-crash is required. The final rapid is an enjoyable class II run with several chutes to choose from.

Lewis Lake is unduly rocky and, unlike the river, has many decent campsites. The exit from Lewis is past three class III-IV rapids but fortunately they all have short portages. Shortly past the last rapid the Assapan River enters from the right. On the map this is marked

Matawa Place, which means "meeting." The high clay banks here are topped with a jack pine plateau. It seems like a natural meeting place.

Do a lift-over at Neekik Rapids, then take-out to scout the next rapids. I call this Notch Rapids because of the small gap or "notch" between the islands. All the channels here look runnable but I opted for the centre one, as it appeared to have deeper water. Using this route leads to an obscured ledge past the first island. With a quick 120 degree turn you can cut back and squeeze through the notch between the two bigger islands, safely exiting the rapid and eluding the ledge and its standing wave.

The first of the Kitchi Rapids is a long class III-IV with no discernible portage. However, it is easily lined if the souse holes in the centre of the river are avoided. The second Kitchi Rapid is a double waterfall with the portage located on river right. A very nice campsite can be found at the base of the falls.

After this strenuous section, the remainder of the river to Harrop Lake is a placid paddle past some interesting rock formations.

The left channel to Harrop Lake, although difficult to locate because it is concealed by vegetation and characteristically located on the edge of the map, is preferred as it leaves you less exposed to weather on the lake. The waterfall at the entrance to Harrop surprisingly has no campsites and none were found until the northeast side of the lake was reached.

Leaving Harrop Lake you again find three class III rapids in quick succession. This time the first two can be run, with caution as the drops are steeper than they appear. However, the third must be portaged and both sides of the river are equally difficult. The river twists away from these rapids before straightening as it enters a narrow scenic canyon for the final two kilometres to Kinkokay Rapids.

A recent fire has eradicated the portage at the class III-IV Kinkokay and the deadfall makes lining precarious. Scramble over, through and around the underbrush for 200 paces past this narrow, steep-walled rapid. The remaining rapids before Wrong Lake are all class I, giving you the opportunity to admire the towering cliffs as you sweep past. Watch for a pictograph on river right as you pass Assinika River.

The fishing lodge, on the left as you enter Wrong Lake, has to be one of the most luxurious in Manitoba. Too fancy a palace for itinerant canoeists, even the

picnic sites come equipped with barbecue pits and tables. One of the nicer ones is on the island at the narrows about halfway down the lake. Legend has it that a survey party arriving at this large lake thought they had reached Lake Winnipeg. Later, realizing their mistake, they named it Wrong Lake.

The Wrong to Weaver Lake section of the Poplar commences with an imposing six metre-high waterfall, the first of many. It has a short but easy portage, leading to a picturesque campsite. This section of the river has either easy rapids or arduous waterfalls. The most memorable feature is the imposing cliff face located about four kilometres downstream from Kawtootookuk Rapids. It looks ready-made for pictographs but none were found, although several were located nearby. The creators of the pictographs must have felt, as I did, that this was a sacred place and should not be despoiled with human artifacts.

In 1989 a scorching fire, between Wathintayappikowin Rapids and the McPhail River, burned the forest to bare rock. Never have I seen such a dearth of vegetation or unappealing campsites. Conversely portaging the falls, unencumbered by brush, was never easier or more obvious. Perhaps it was too obvious as at Akik Rapids the put-in on the left was very steep and river right was a better, albeit

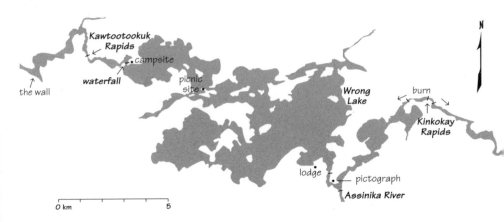

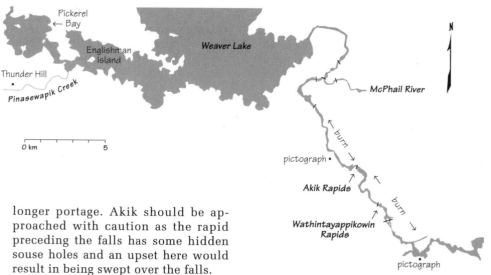

longer portage. Akik should be approached with caution as the rapid preceding the falls has some hidden souse holes and an upset here would result in being swept over the falls.

The McPhail River with its picturesque waterfall and small campsite marks the end of the intense 1989 fire. Evidence of an older fire is occasionally seen along the shoreline. There is one more class III, then a quick four kilometre paddle through a swampy area to Weaver Lake.

Weaver is the largest lake on the Poplar River and the most direct route involves a seven kilometre paddle across the exposed middle of the lake. This is followed by an additional seven kilometre traverse of the relatively narrower western end and concludes with a three kilometre crossing of Pickerel Bay. Since this will take a minimum of three-and-a-half hours, prudence suggests that a crossing not be commenced after noon and a period of light winds be waited for.

Weaver Lake has many intriguing landmarks. Pinasewapik Creek leads, with difficulty, to Pinasewapik or Thunder Hill. Ascending the creek can be a struggle, but the view from the hill is worth the effort. Set aside a day for this hike and leave the heavy packs at camp. Legend has it that the mythical thunderbirds nested on this hill. Located directly across the lake from Pinasewapik Creek is a flat point with a

sand beach ideal for camping. The large island a kilometre to the west is known as Englishman Island, suggesting that the Hudson's Bay Co. had a trading post here. An HBC map of 1819 shows both a Hudson's Bay Co. and a North West Co. post at Thunder Lake, as it was then known, in 1806-07. The steep-sided Englishman Island may well have been chosen for a trading post because of its defensive features.

At Moniakatiksechink Island keep to the left channel as Sakitawonk Rapids, a class III-IV, can be lined. There is a waterfall in the centre channel and the right channel can only be used at very high water levels.

At the next rapid, which I call Hobson's Choice, an island splits the river. Both sides are equally interesting but present different challenges. On the left there is a class III narrow, steep canyon. The steep sides make lining difficult and since no portage was found the rapid must be run. The right side has a waterfall with an established portage river left where the canoes can slide along the rock. Obviously most canoeists choose the right but the left is tempting. If only I didn't have the food packs!

The distance from Hobson's Choice to Kawawakechewonk Rapids is 13 kilometres, through attractive rocky country with only short bits of fast water. Kawawakechewonk is a triple set: the first two are class I and the third is a class II-III with a short lift-over, if necessary. It is only 1.5 kilometres to Wapinnonik Rapids—a long class II that can be portaged on either side. This is followed by another 10 kilometres of rocky shoreline culminating in the finest rapid on the Poplar, Nantuko, or as I call it, Surfing Rapid.

Surfing is another long class II with several possible lines and finishing with a small ledge, creating an unblemished standing wave for its entire 25 metre length. An easy portage and idyllic campsite complete this perfect setting. We couldn't resist camping here and spending the remainder of the day running the rapid and surfing the wave.

From Surfing Rapid it is only a few hours paddle to the town of Poplar River, with only one portage at the waterfall at Onakuyam. Below the falls there is a large eddy full of logs, implying that log drives still occur. A road and boat launch, bypassing the falls, provide access for townspeople to the upper river.

The town has grown substantially since the topographical map was printed, with a new bridge crossing the river at the narrows. Continue downstream until you reach the ferry dock on river right. The Northern store is close to the dock and the airport is a short walk away. If desired the store manager can arrange to have your canoe shipped to Selkirk and you can catch a flight to Winnipeg.

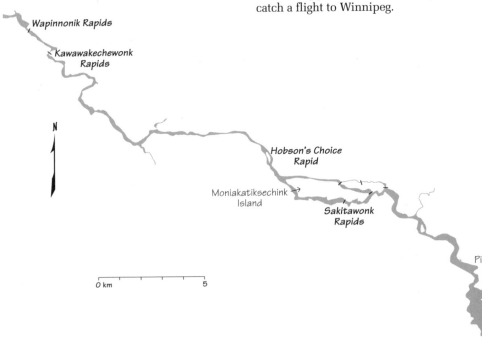

Wapinnonik Rapids

Kawawakechewonk Rapids

N

Hobson's Choice Rapid

Moniakatiksechink Island

Sakitawonk Rapids

0 km   5

Pic B

Thunder Hill

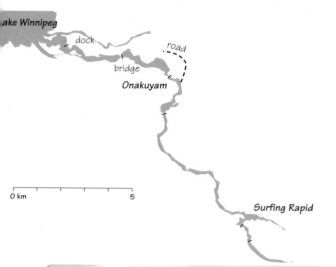

Onakuyam

Surfing Rapid

Wapinnonik → Rapids

Peruvian Quinoa Stew

It seems appropriate to have a vegetarian dish on a river named after a tree such as the Poplar River.

Servings: 4

1/2 cup quinoa
2 cups onions
2 garlic cloves
2 tb vegetable oil
1 celery stalk
1 carrot
1 green pepper
1 cup zucchini
2 cups tomatoes
2 ts cumin
1/2 ts chili powder
1 ts coriander
1 pinch cayenne
1 ts oregano
salt to taste
1/2 cup cilantro
1 cup cheddar

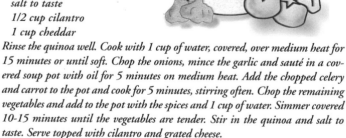

Rinse the quinoa well. Cook with 1 cup of water, covered, over medium heat for 15 minutes or until soft. Chop the onions, mince the garlic and sauté in a covered soup pot with oil for 5 minutes on medium heat. Add the chopped celery and carrot to the pot and cook for 5 minutes, stirring often. Chop the remaining vegetables and add to the pot with the spices and 1 cup of water. Simmer covered 10-15 minutes until the vegetables are tender. Stir in the quinoa and salt to taste. Serve topped with cilantro and grated cheese.

Rice River

Type Small wilderness flatwater river
Difficulty Beginner
Distance 13 km
Time 1 day
Access Turn north at the winter road 8.3 km east of Manigotagan on Hwy. #304. Follow the winter road for 30 km to the bridge crossing Rice River. There is good parking on the south side of the bridge.
Topo Maps 62P7, 62P8
Season June to September. Best in July.

From the put-in below the rapids paddle downstream to Lake Winnipeg. There is one small class I rapid near the mouth that can be run river left. The river empties into Lake Winnipeg at the south end of the Kasakeemeemisekak islands, an archipelago of small islands and rocky outcrops. This archipelago plus adjacent Deer and Black islands have been nominated as a component of the proposed Interlake National Park representing the Manitoba Lowlands. It is the most biologically diverse area in the lowlands and home to several rare (in Manitoba) species such as the Caspian tern and red pine.

Upon reaching the lake, it is advisable to paddle straight east until the outer islands are reached. Leave a marker on one of the islands because the river can be very hard to locate on the return journey. Even bet-

ter, carry a Global Positioning Systems (GPS) receiver and note the location of the river mouth. A GPS is also important to determine your location in the web of islands, bays and promontories. From the river mouth it is about 6.5 kilometres across the open lake to Deer Island with its miles of deserted beaches and geologically interesting beach ridges. Explore the beach for animal tracks and shells. If the lake is too rough to paddle turn north and canoe in the shelter of the Kasakeemeemisekak Islands. The islands stretch for about 10 kilometres along the shore of the lake, offering many excellent camping spots. This is a birder's paradise with hundreds of pelicans, blue herons, cranes, cormorants, terns, gulls, geese and grebes soaring overhead. Swim, fish or just relax and enjoy the solitude before turning your canoe around and heading home.

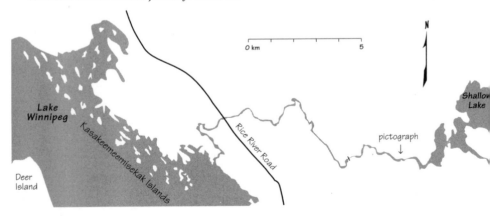

Every rocky protrusion contains some nesting sites, but the largest concentration is on the Pipestone Rocks, a bird sanctuary about three kilometres north of Deer Island. Here colonies of pelicans, cormorants and terns nest together in a cacophony of sound. To minimize your impact never land on the islands and wait till the end of June to visit when the chicks are ready to leave the nests.

An alternative trip is to paddle upstream to Shallow Lake—a distance of 13 kilometres from the bridge. As you paddle past low rock outcrops and jack pine forest you will have to portage 12 rapids. The distances are short and the portages easy but you will have to find your own way as there are no trails on this little used river. Just before you reach Shallow Lake watch for a large pictograph site, comparable to the well-known site on the Bloodvein, on the north side.

Shallow Lake is low and swampy and offers few camping spots. Try the second point where the lake opens up to the main body. You can continue upstream to Kapeemechekamak Lake a further 12 kilometres, but I did not explore this part of the river.

Wild Rice Salad

Wild rice is plentiful in the fall on the aptly named Rice River. Gather a few pounds and enjoy this fresh salad all winter to remind you of a Manitoba summer.

Servings: 4
1 cup wild rice
4 cups chicken broth
1 lg orange
1/4 cup fresh mint
4 green onions
1 cup yellow raisins
1 cup pecans
1/4 cup olive oil
salt and pepper to taste

Cook the rice in the chicken stock for 50-60 minutes. Grate, peel and add the juice of the orange. Add the remaining ingredients and let stand for several hours to blend flavours. Salt and pepper to taste and serve at room temperature.

Roseau River

Type Mid-sized fast-flowing river
Difficulty Intermediate
Distance 54 km
Time 1-2 days
Access 11 km south on first section road east of Vita.
Egress Bridge at Hwy. #218.
Topo Maps 62H2, 62H3
Season April to May

The Roseau River in southeastern Manitoba is an unexpected delight. Unlike the Rat and Whitemouth, which flow across swampy terrain, the Roseau has eroded a course through the Sandilands Moraine before entering the Red River plain. Through the moraine the riverbed is composed of gravel and rocks, some of which are a substantial size, that provide a variety of challenges for canoeists. Owing to the early breakup and proximity to Winnipeg, canoeists can be found on the river most weekends in April practising their winter rested whitewater skills.

The Roseau was used by La Verendrye and the North West Company fur traders as an alternate route to Winnipeg, especially in the spring when high water made the Winnipeg River dangerous. The junction of the Roseau and Red rivers was also a renowned meeting place for the Plains Indians who held a feast here each fall.

In 1930 the Gardenton Floodway was built to control flooding in the area. Since then the river channel has dried-up and become overgrown. The floodway runs straight for 10 kilometres before rejoining the original river channel eight kilometres above Gardenton. It has increased peak flows downstream about 20 per cent, a real bonus for canoeists. Usually canoeing in a ditch is monotonous, but this floodway is different. The left bank forms a dike and blocks the view of the farms and fields to the east. The dike is a favourite spot for sandhill cranes in the spring. On the right the land is flat and usually flooded in the spring when the floodway overflows. An excellent waterfowl nesting area, it is frequented by geese, godwits, pintails, mallards and northern shovellers. The strong current confined between narrow banks makes for a relaxing trip in the spring. At lower water levels, boulders are frequently exposed, requiring tricky manoeuvring in some tight quarters.

Laura Bahattacharya on old swinging bridge.

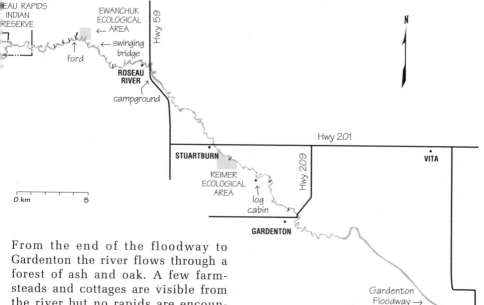

From the end of the floodway to Gardenton the river flows through a forest of ash and oak. A few farmsteads and cottages are visible from the river but no rapids are encountered. At Gardenton the old highway bridge still exists, but Hwy. #209 now crosses the river where the topographical map shows a railway bridge.

After Gardenton the forest gradually gives way to an aspen-oak savannah to past Stuartburn. About halfway to Stuartburn there is an old one-room house on river left built of poplar logs and faced with branches covered with dried mud. This material was called white mud and was commonly used by homesteaders to build houses. In this section, there are three easy rapids to negotiate, the final one requiring some manoeuvring. Past the last rapid there is a picnic site on river left with access to the 75 hectare Reimer Ecological Significant Area of aspen and oak prairie that has never been broken. Take the time to tramp around the area and discover native prairie plants blooming in their natural environment.

Leaving Stuartburn, there are several shallow, rocky rapids in the first few kilometres. Then the river flows swiftly and without obstructions to Hwy. #59. Summer residences are common along this part of the river. A campground one

kilometre before the town of Roseau River has picnic tables and toilets. This is a good place for lunch or to commence a day trip.

From the Roseau River bridge to the ford the river is very rocky and there are frequent rapids and turbulence. This is the favoured part of the river for whitewater boaters. They can be found here enjoying the first paddle of the year from early April until the water levels drop too low for canoeing. There are two swinging bridges crossing the river. Care is needed to pass them when the water is high and the current strong. The first one is located about five kilometres from Hwy. #59 and is apparently still used.

The second swinging bridge is another 3.5 kilometres downstream and is no longer in use. It is located on a tight bend of the river and can't be seen until it is almost too late to avoid. It was apparently designed for parishioners to cross the river and attend church on Sunday mornings.

Abandoned swinging bridge in early spring.

Swinging bridge.

The ford is a favourite place to stop for lunch. You can get a good view of the river from the top of the hill. The property on the north side of the river is a deciduous forest and sedge meadow that the owner has voluntarily protected as an Ecological Significant Area.

The longest and most difficult rapids on the river are found between the ford and Roseau Rapids Indian Reserve. Here the river again becomes very rocky and turbulent. At the reserve the Roseau enters the flat Red River valley with its thick clay deposits that are the legacy of glacial Lake Agassiz. As expected, the Roseau becomes a typical slow, meandering prairie river with low muddy banks. The deep rich soil can support much larger and a greater variety of trees than can grow in the poorer soils upstream. Substantial cottonwoods can be found along the river. Occasionally these huge trees are undermined and topple into the river, virtually blocking the passage and requiring deft manoeuvring to avoid.

Hwy. #218 is the recommended finishing spot for canoe trips on the Roseau. It is a long day's paddle from Hwy. #59. Past Hwy. #218 the river is sluggish meandering and many farmyards run down to the river. The next possible egress is a bridge about 10 kilometres downstream by river or five kilometres by road, demonstrating how much distance meanders can add.

Arthur's Porridge

The Roseau River is best in April when both the water and the wind are cold. A bowl of this steaming hot porridge will warm you up and keep you going all day. It is no comparison to that gruel your mother fed you every morning.

Servings: 14
4 cups bran flakes
3 cups rolled oats
2 cups triticale flakes
1 cup barley flakes
1 cup wheat flakes
2 cups cracked oats
2 cups cracked wheat
1 cup pot barley (whole barley)
1 cup oat groats (whole oats)
1/2 cup flax seed
pinch of salt
1 handful raisins
milk and brown sugar

Mix all the grains thoroughly in a large container. Store in wide mouth jars or plastic bags.

At camp, for each serving, bring 1 cup of water to a boil. Add a pinch of salt, a handful of raisins and 1 cup of porridge mix. Stir and cover. Turn the stove to lowest heat and let the porridge stand for 5 minutes. Serve with milk and brown sugar.

Sasaginnigak River

Type Wilderness
Difficulty Beginner
Distance 23 km
Time 1 Day
Access By plane to Sasaginnigak Lake.
Egress Via the Bloodvein River.
Topo Maps 52M12
Season June to September

The Sasaginnigak River flows 23 kilometres from its source at Sasaginnigak Lake to its junction with the Bloodvein River. It is the easiest way into the Sasaginnigak and Family Lake area and the numerous rivers flowing out of these lakes. The Sasaginnigak is a narrow river flowing through an area of low relief. The aspen woodlands of the upper section give way to a tamarack bog and swamp before the Bloodvein junction. Wild rice grows in abundance along the shore, providing food for the waterfowl who nest along the river. The rapids act as dams maintaining the water levels in between.

Following my usual practise I will describe the river from source to mouth although it is most frequently paddled in the opposite direction. Sasaginnigak Lake is a large lake with many beautiful islands. An open rocky shoreline provides many excellent campsites. The rocky terrain continues to the second rapid where it gives way to the aspen woodlands characteristic of this river.

The first rapid is a class I-II with a 170-pace portage on river left that goes over a high rock. There is a good campsite at the top. The first portage is just around the corner where a class III rapid

Author canoeing in low water. Photo: Gerry Reckseidler.

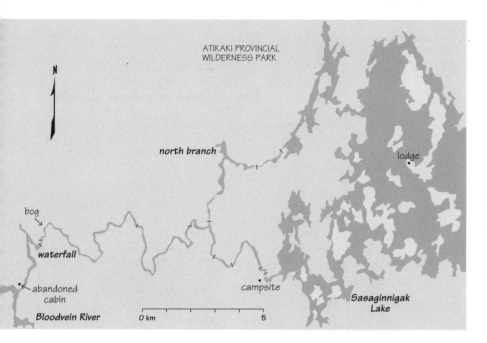

is encountered leading to two small ledges. The short portage on river left gives ample opportunity for scouting.

A class I- precedes a long, shallow, unmarked class III-IV rapid with a massive pile of debris at the end. The portage is 270 paces on river right. The riverbed here is a large, smooth sheet of rock on which a few huge square-edged boulders have been scattered like a giant discarding a building block set.

For the next 12 kilometres the river winds its way through dense stands of poplar, and wild rice grows in profusion along the shore. Two class I rapids are encountered, with the latter having a 90-pace portage on river left. Between these two rapids the north branch of the river enters via a picturesque waterfall. The final rapid is a class II-III. The small ledge at here can be portaged on river left and the remainder run or the 170-pace portage on river right can be used to bypass both. Watch for the eagle nest on river left as you exit the rapid.

The terrain slowly changes from marsh to a tamarack bog and finally a floating bog. The six metre-high waterfall two kilometres before the Bloodvein comes as a surprise in this flat country. The 100-pace portage is on river right through heavy brush. The falls here are worth a visit as you can walk along the open rock next to them.

On river right at the junction of the Bloodvein high above the river there is the remains of an old cabin. It is reputed to have been built by a free trader who lived in the area in the 1930s. Poke around the area and speculate on how he lived in this harsh climate and what his daily routine must have been like. The presence of a trader suggests that the area supported a reasonable population. Archaeological finds from several sites in the area date human occupation from about 1000 AD.

Brazilian Peanut Stew

I learned this recipe from my son after his South America trip. I first tried it on my canoeing partner, Gerry, on a cool September evening on the Sasaginnigak River. Gerry likes his food spicy and recommends that you leave the chillies in for flavour.

Servings: 4
1 lg onion
4 sm garlic cloves
1 tb paprika
2 sm dried hot chillies
4 tb olive oil
28 oz canned tomatoes
1/4 ts cayenne pepper
1/4 ts ginger
1/4 ts nutmeg
1/4 ts cinnamon ground
1 cup coconut milk
1/2 cup peanut butter
1 cup black bean flakes
1 cup corn
1-1/2 cups brown rice
dash of salt
peanuts

At home, chop the onion and garlic (dry if desired) and package together. Package the paprika and chillies together. Package the remaining ingredients together, drying as necessary.

At camp, heat the oil in a pot with the paprika and chillies. After 3-5 minutes discard the chillies. Add the onion and garlic and sauté. Add the tomatoes, seasonings and 1 cup of water to the pot. Simmer for 15-20 minutes. Blend the coconut milk and peanut butter until smooth, then add to the pot, stirring until incorporated. Add the black bean flakes and corn. Add water as required to maintain desired consistency. Simmer 15 minutes.

While the stew is simmering, cook the brown rice. Bring 2 cups of water to a boil. Stir in the rice and a dash of salt. Return to a boil. Cover and simmer for 5 minutes. Remove from the heat, stir and let sit covered for 5 minutes. Fluff and serve.

Serve the stew hot over rice and garnish with peanuts.

Shell River

Type Small rocky river
Difficulty Beginner
Distance 12 km/47 km from Hwy. #5
Time 1 day
Access Two km east on section road, 6.5 km north of Shell River on Hwy. #83.
Egress Asessippi Provincial Park.
Topo Maps 62K14 and 62N3
Season May

For most of its journey from the Duck Mountains to the Assiniboine, the Shell River is a small creek. It meanders across the broad, flat valley and rich farmlands between the Duck and Riding mountains. This part of the river is characterized by low banks thickly overgrown with a narrow band of willow backed by open pasture. Only the final 12 kilometres where the river drops 30 metres down to the Assiniboine River valley provide scenic and enjoyable canoeing. Although short, this river is rich in historical associations.

From the put-in to Asessippi Provincial Park the river flows through a narrow, heavily-wooded valley. The hills rise up to 90 metres above the river and in places are very steep. Mature poplar and aspen with a thick understory of hazelnut and Manitoba maple provide habitat for a multiplicity of birds. Ninety-three species have been identified in the valley including abundant populations of the Yellow-throated vireo, which is rare in Manitoba. There are no waterfalls to portage and obstacles like sweepers are uncommon. In 1993 only one fence line was found crossing the river. Appropriately, the riverbed in many places is densely littered with clam shells. Hawks, osprey and cormorants are abundant along the river, perhaps attracted by the shells.

On the topographical map the Shell looks like a railway line because there are so many rapids marked. Fortunately, they are all class I or II's, but much

longer than the ledges common in the Precambrian Shield rivers of Manitoba. Even the rocks are smaller than the boulders often found in other rivers.

River access at the put-in is complicated by barbed wire strung to all four corners of the bridge, presumably to keep cattle away from the river. There are two rapids separated by the timbers of a former bridge just downstream from the put-in.

There are virtually continuous rapids or rocky shoals for the next 3.5 kilometres. A brief respite from the rapids allows you to relax and watch the landscape flow past. This is predominately a cattle ranching area but few signs of agriculture are visible from the river. After a kilometre of quiet paddling, the river resumes its headlong descent into the valley and the rapids begin again and continue until Hwy. #83 is reached.

At Hwy. #83, Inglis Lions Club Park is located on the left side of the river. Picnic tables and a small beach make an inviting lunch spot and provide a chance for a refreshing swim. A concealed sheet metal dam blocks the river here and necessitates a portage on river left. At flows greater than five cubic metres per second this could be a dangerous obstacle as a hidden "keeper" could be formed by the water flowing over the dam.

Below the dam, the Shell River is noticeably shallower. The river winds more and behaves like a typical prairie river as it leaves shallow sand beaches on the inside of bends while carving into the steep hills on the outside.

There is a surprising sight one kilometre past Hwy. #83, an old steel truss bridge on the bank of the river. The bridge was obviously built to support trains. Why it was used to carry light vehicle traffic across the Shell is a mystery. The original stone masonry bridge supports still exist suggesting that the bridge was installed about 1900. On the embankment above the river here there are two well-preserved but abandoned houses. This is all that remains of the town of Asessippi. The town was founded in 1882 and flourished briefly with the construction of a dam, flour mill, saw-mill and cheese factory, but the promised railway line never arrived and Asessippi faded away. This is an inter-esting place to explore and to specu-late on the lives of the residents.

It is reported that the sawmill used logs from the Duck Mountains, which were floated down the river in the spring. If true, the spring floods must have been a sight to behold.

Shortly after leaving the ghostly Asessippi, you arrive at the old Hwy. #83 bridge where the river enters the Lake of the Prairies. It is about three kilometres farther to the beach and marina at Asessippi Provincial Park where you will find camping, a concession serving cold drinks and tables. The Lake of the Prairies is reputed to have the best pickerel fishing in Manitoba. This, rather than the shells, likely accounts for the abundance of os-prey and cormorants.

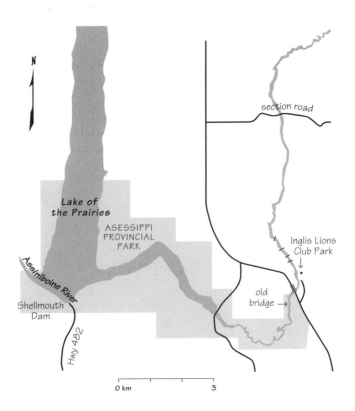

New Mex Stroganoff

This is an excellent meal for the Shell River as all the ingredients can be left in a cooler in camp until needed. If you find this worth preparing away from refrigeration substitute dried mushrooms and a package of sour cream.

Servings: 4

1 lb button mushrooms, sliced
1/8 oz porcine mushrooms
1/2 ts thyme
1/2 ts basil
3 tb parsley, minced
2 tb chives, minced
1 onion, diced
3 tb olive oil
3 tb flour
1/4 cup white wine
3/4 cup vegetable stock or water
1 clove garlic
2 tb Hungarian paprika
2 ts chili powder
1 pkg sour cream mix
salt and pepper to taste
1 lb noodles

At home, dry the mushrooms, thyme, basil, parsley and chives. At camp, sauté the onion in oil for 1 minute. Add the mushrooms and continue cooking. Toss with flour until the mixture is evenly coated. Add the wine and stock or water, stirring until thick. Reduce heat to simmer and add garlic, thyme, basil, paprika and chili powder. Cover and simmer 15 minutes. Add parsley, chive and sour cream mix, stirring thoroughly. Do not boil. Add salt and pepper to taste. Serve over noodles.

Souris River

Type Mid-sized flatwater river
Difficulty Beginner
Distance 58 km
Time 2-3 days
Access Bridge on Hwy. #348, nine km south of Hwy. #2.
Egress Confluence of Assiniboine River.
Topo Maps 62F9, 62G5, 62G12
Season April to June

The Souris River arises in Saskatchewan, dips into North Dakota, and returns to Canada in Manitoba where it eventually joins the Assiniboine southeast of Brandon. All the political jurisdictions want a share of the water for industrial or agricultural purposes, so the flow of the Souris is much diminished by the time it reaches the Assiniboine. As a result, the best time to paddle it is very early in the spring to take advantage of the spring runoff. Unfortunately, the trees have not leafed out and most flowers are not yet in bloom so the river environment is still cloaked in drab winter colours. If water levels allow, the best time to travel the river is in early May to catch the end of bird migration and the brilliant greens of the first spring blooms.

As it enters Manitoba, the Souris flows through a broad valley carved by a huge meltwater river. This valley was created by the waters draining from the face of retreating glaciers. These glacier rivers deposited the deep layers of alluvial till that today are the farmlands along the river. Southeast of Souris the river enters the Manitoba Escarpment, an area of grey shale that was not significantly eroded by glaciation. Here the river has carved deep canyons in the shale banks

Line up at Zap's Corner.

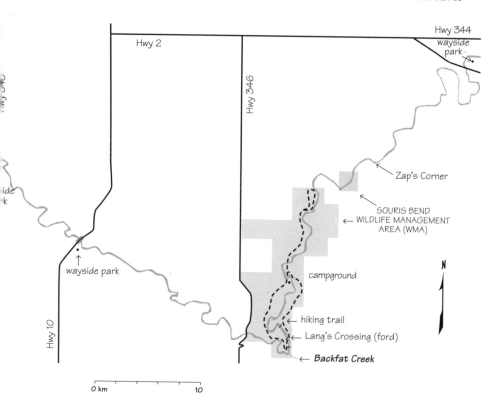

as it drops 30 metres in 34 kilometres. By Wawanesa, the escarpment has been traversed and the remaining few kilometres cross the sandy delta of the Assiniboine River.

When the present course of the Souris was blocked by glacial ice, it drained east through the present-day Pembina Valley. About 8,000 years ago the Souris was diverted north by a tongue of glacial ice into the Assiniboine. This region, where the river turns abruptly north, is known as the Souris Bend.

From the Manitoba border to Hwy. #348 the Souris flows through a wide valley dominated by grainfields. Irrigation pumps, control dams and barbed wire fences combine to make this section of the river unsuitable for canoeing. The Manitoba Escarpment with its steep banks discourages agricultural usage

and the steeper gradient makes the lower part of the Souris a canoeist's delight. It is the finest river in southwestern Manitoba with scenery, rapids and wildlife on display for the canoeist.

At the Hwy. #348 access there is a wayside park on the southwest side of the bridge, but the best parking and canoe put-in is on the northeast corner. From Hwy. #348 to Hwy. #346 there are numerous short stretches of fast water and easy rapids. These easy rapids provide good practise for the more difficult sets beyond the Souris Bend. The Souris Bend Wildlife Management Area is entered at Hwy. #346. This 2,082 ha Wildlife Management Area straddles the river for the next 13 kilometres protecting wildlife habitat, particularly deer. Besides canoeing, the Wildlife Management Area offers hiking and biking opportunities. Campsites have been established, with one, at Lang's

Crossing, accessible by canoe. Hwy. #346 can be used as a starting point for an interesting, if long, day trip.

Entering the Tiger Hills east of Hwy. #10 the riverbanks get progressively higher, eventually towering 75 metres above the river at the Souris Bend. Here the river turns north leaving the ancient meltwater river channel to carve a narrow, deep ravine through the Tiger Hills to the Assiniboine River. For the next five kilometres there are frequent class I rapids as the river flows over a series of shallow gravel bars. The few boulders and absence of ledges make these rapids a joy to play in for experienced canoeists and they are easily navigated by novices.

The shale cliffs rise vertically from the river to heights of 75 metres. Besides being awe inspiring, they present a rare opportunity to study an unusual aspect of Manitoba history. Piles of buffalo bones have been found at the base of some cliffs, suggesting that native hunt-

ers stampeded the animals over the edge. Fossils and mammoth bones have also been found, as well as pottery and tool remains. The scarcity of human dwellings intensifies the feeling of being in the wilderness and enhances the sense of paddling through history.

About 11 kilometres before Hwy. #2 the character of the river changes when it leaves the Tiger Hills and enters the Assiniboine River delta. The river meanders through a low floodplain dominated by oak. Undercuts and sweepers are more frequent and can easily trap the unwary paddler.

Day trips usually end at the wayside park on the northeast side of the bridge at Hwy. #2. Secluded parking and short trails to explore partially compensate for the difficult egress and make this a pleasant place to await the car shuttle. However, it is only another eight kilometres more to Wawanesa. Here the Lions Park on river right offers more

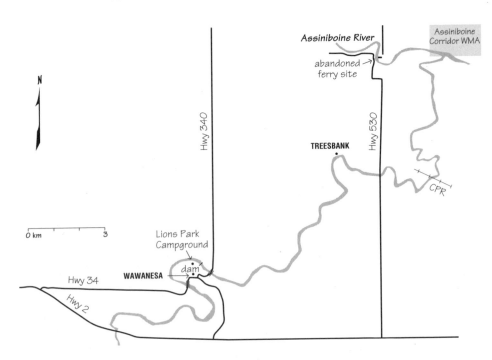

Early spring.

amenities while awaiting the car shuttle. Picnicking or camping in the fully-serviced campground is also available and a coffee shop is nearby. Look for the inconspicuous dam obstructing the river at the park. Since a portage is necessary anyhow, plan to take a break at this restful spot. If continuing downriver, Lions Park is the best campsite before the Assiniboine.

From Wawanesa to the Assiniboine there is 21 kilometres of peaceful paddling. No rapids are encountered and the high banks maintain the picturesque qualities of the river until Hwy. #530. Past the bridge, sandbars start appearing in the river and the Assiniboine is soon reached.

Three choices are available at the confluence to reach an egress point. The first choice is to paddle three kilometres upstream against the usually slow current of the Assiniboine to the site of the former Treesbank ferry where a road runs down on either side of the river. The second alternative is to continue downstream on the Assiniboine 18 kilometres to the Stockton ferry or a further 35 kilometres to Hwy. #5 at Spruce Woods Provincial Park. The final option is to cross

the Assiniboine and scale the 15 banks on the north side. A short distance north there is a dirt road that winds for three kilometres through the mixed-grass prairie to a gravel road that connects with Hwy. #340. If you choose this option be prepared for a long wait for the car shuttle, but studying the plants and exploring this Wildlife Management Area will make the time pass quickly.

Overview from hiking trail.

Elegant Mouse

The Souris is French for mouse, and although I have never found them worse than on other rivers, all those hawks circling over the fields are feeding on something.

> *Servings: 4*
> *1 cup mouse, fresh if possible*
> *1 tb oil*
> *1/2 cup peas, dried*
> *4 tb chicken bouillon*
> *1 ts dill weed*
> *3 cups pasta*
> *2 1/2 tb onion soup mix*
> *1 tb milk powder*
> *1 pkg sour cream mix*

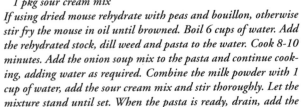

If using dried mouse rehydrate with peas and bouillon, otherwise stir fry the mouse in oil until browned. Boil 6 cups of water. Add the rehydrated stock, dill weed and pasta to the water. Cook 8-10 minutes. Add the onion soup mix to the pasta and continue cooking, adding water as required. Combine the milk powder with 1 cup of water, add the sour cream mix and stir thoroughly. Let the mixture stand until set. When the pasta is ready, drain, add the sour cream to the pot and stir.

If mice are in short supply, you can substitute chicken. It tastes almost as good.

Valley River

Type Small pastoral river
Difficulty Intermediate
Distance 58 km
Time 2-3 days
Access Bridge on Hwy. #274 two km north of Gilbert Plains.
Egress Bridge on Hwy. #362 at the town of Valley River.
Topo Maps 62N1 and 62N8
Season April to June

The Valley River arises in the swamps and bogs of Duck Mountain Park, drains the south side of the Duck, flows through a broad valley between the Duck and Riding mountains, and finally crosses the flat shoreline of Dauphin Lake. Above Grandview the Valley is a small, weedy, meandering creek of little interest to canoeists. Beyond the town of Valley River the river meanders for 40 kilometres across flat meadows to Dauphin Lake. Only the 60 kilometre stretch between Gilbert Plains and Valley River where the river crosses the Manitoba Escarpment is of interest to the canoeist.

Although lacking the deep canyons of the Souris and the challenging rapids of the Whitemouth, the Valley has an abundant variety of wildlife and long, rocky class I rapids that test your abilities to find the main channel.

Beavers are the most frequently seen animal on the Valley. There seems to be a beaver dam every few kilometres and always at the top of a rapid. In times of high water these dams are not a problem as the canoes slide easily over top, but in low water dragging the canoes over or around the numerous dams would soon become tedious and add many hours to a journey.

Beaver dam.

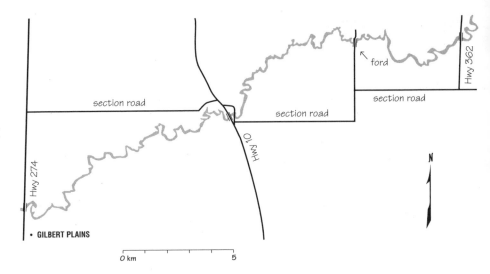

At Gilbert Plains the river is narrow and fast with banks up to 4.5 metres high. The soil is sandy loam and evergreens predominate. The water is surprisingly clear but signs of cattle on shore suggest the water should not be consumed. From Hwy. #274 to Hwy. #10 there are frequent long, rocky rapids usually preceded by a beaver dam. The rapids are mostly class I but interesting in that there are frequent rocks to avoid and little room to manoeuvre in the narrow channel. The high wooded banks screen the adjoining cultivated lands from view and give the canoeist a sense of being in the wilderness. Surprisingly, unlike many other rivers in rural Manitoba, no debris or garbage dumps were found along the river.

At Hwy. #10 the landscape changes. The banks are lower but still heavily wooded with ash, oak and aspen predominating rather than evergreens. Farming is more evident although still unobtrusive. More importantly, the rapids become small drops over ledges with fewer rocks rather than the long runs found above Hwy. #10. The rapids marked on the topographical map were not found.

The ford marked on the map has been replaced with a low concrete dam that necessitates a portage. The ford is a good egress point for a shorter trip or a day-trip from Hwy. #10. From the ford to Hwy. #362 there are few rapids and little fast water. After the ford, the river often separates into several channels around grassy islands any of which could be the main channel. The footbridge marked on the topographical map was not seen in 1993 and only one fence-line was found crossing the river.

If time permits visit Trembowla nine kilometres north on Hwy. #491 and view the many historic buildings including St. Michael's church, the site of the first Ukrainian Catholic Mass held in Canada.

The Valley is an excellent river for learning to paddle rapids as it is very forgiving. It has superb wildlife viewing in a wilderness setting and yet is always close to assistance if required.

Jambalaya

This flavourful one pot meal is a favourite on the Valley River because there are no portages and weight is not a problem.

Servings: 4
1-1/2 cups instant brown rice
6 tb margarine
1 can ham flakes
1 can chicken flakes
1 can shrimp
16 oz tomato paste
2 pkg Cajun King Jambalaya seasoning

At home, sauté the rice in the margarine and package in a waterproof bag. Add dry ham, chicken and shrimp. At camp, add the tomato paste to 1 cup of water and boil. Blend the jambalaya seasoning in 2 cups of water. Combine all the ingredients and simmer in a tightly covered pot until the liquid is absorbed and the rice is fluffy. Remove from heat and let sit covered for 10 minutes.

Wanipigow River

Type Small wilderness river
Difficulty Intermediate
Distance 90 km
Time 2-4 days
Access Campground at Wallace Lake 30 Km east of Bissett on Hwy. #304.
Egress Winter road bridge 10 km east of Manigotagan and five km north off Hwy. #304.
Topo Maps 52L14, 52M3, 52M4, 62P1
Season June to September

The Wanipigow is a small river in eastern Manitoba that forms the southern border of Atikaki Provincial Wilderness Park. As with most small rivers, it is often difficult to canoe because of low water. Unlike the larger Manigotagan just a few miles south, in the past the Wanipigow was seldom used as an access to the interior, at least not above Wanipigow Lake. A rarely used river with a wilderness park on the north shore provides an excellent opportunity for experiencing nature in a pristine environment.

From the headwaters—an unnamed lake a kilometre from the Manitoba-Ontario border to Siderock Lake—the Wanipigow follows a narrow, rocky trench where it is often possible to touch both sides of the river. This section is sometimes easier to wade than to paddle.

The largest island at the east end of Siderock has a large, well-used campsite. This site is often used as a starting point for the Obukowin portage.

From Siderock to Wallace Lake the Wanipigow contorts its way through seven kilometres of interminable

Beaver dam at junction of Broadleaf River.

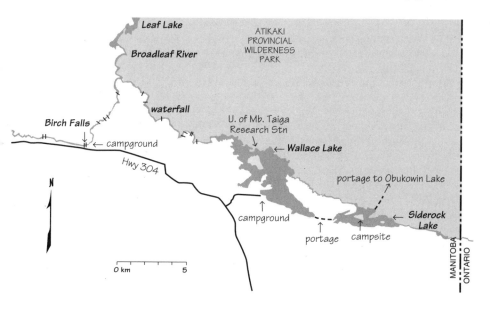

swamp. Most canoeists choose the 1.5 kilometre-long portage found at the west end of the lake. Even though it is long it is very flat, dry and well marked, whereas the Wanipigow River wanders aimlessly through a swamp before reaching Wallace Lake. The portage is usually the quickest of the two routes, even double carrying.

Wallace Lake has road access, a campground, many cottages and a lot of burn. In the 1980s this area suffered several forest fires. There is less burn and consequently better camping and fewer boats at the north end of the lake.

It is about 30 kilometres from Wallace Lake to Birch Falls wayside park. The river is shallow, narrow and shows little use. There is a lot of swamp, some wild rice patches and little camping except at the rapids, which are narrow clefts in granite outcrops and offer little chance for manoeuvring. They are mostly short, rocky runs either class I or less or class III or better.

A kilometre after leaving Wallace Lake there are four easily run short rapids, with no apparent portages, spaced out in the next kilometre. Two kilometres of typical Wanipigow swamp past the fourth rapid there is a waterfall. This 1.5 metre drop is portaged on river left. The next two rapids are also portaged, the last one being one of those enticing almost-runnables. It would likely be an easy run in high water, if there was ever high water in this river.

It is another 2.5 kilometres to the Broadleaf River, which reportedly has more beaver dams than any other river in Manitoba. This accounts for the niggardly flow often found at the confluence. The topographical map here is confusing as it appears the river goes north when in fact it continues west.

Shortly after passing the Broadleaf there is an unmarked class I and then still more of the Wanipigow's seemingly endless supply of swamp for another two kilometres. The next three rapids are marked on the map as doubles and they all require portaging. They follow a common pattern by starting with a serious drop and finishing with a trickle through a rock garden. The portages, when they can be found, are animal trails through alder thickets and deadfall.

Finally, two kilometres of pleasant paddling leads to two class I rapids that are runnable at most water levels—a little reward for persevering this far. Located at the end of the last rapid is Birch Falls wayside park up the steep hill on river left. From here to Wanipigow Lake the river is even narrower and full of deadfall. It is easier to hike this section than paddle it. Unless you are into serious masochism, portage the next section by car to Currie's Landing park, 11 kilometres west of Bissett and close to Wanipigow Lake. Continuing the trip

from here should save at least two day's paddling. Currie's Landing is so named after Donald Currie who carried freight from here to Bissett and Long Lake.

Wanipigow Lake is a long, narrow lake with two campgrounds on the south shore but no other developments. It is a typical shield lake. A control dam at the east end of the lake reduces the flow, usually to a mere trickle. A boat ramp and road access make this an inviting egress. Located below the dam are three rapids within half a kilometre with no portages and usually no water. Past the Rice River bridge there are two more difficult rapids before Clangula Lake. From Clangula to Lake Winnipeg the river is marshy.

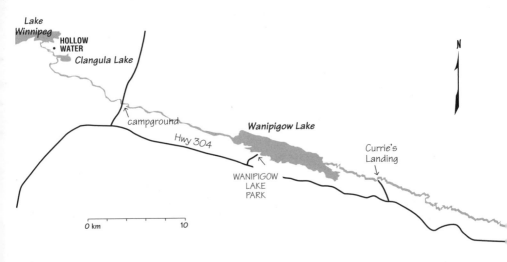

Author paddling in Wanipigow swamp. Photo: Jack Armstrong.

Hot Pot

A hot, spicy meal for frequent cool sping days on the Wanipigow River.
Servings: 4
1-1/2 cups chicken, dried
1/2 cup tomatoes, dried
1 pkg corn, dried
1/4 cup mushrooms, dried
1 pkg chili seasoning mix
1 pkg corn chips
4 oz cheddar cheese

Rehydrate the chicken and vegetables. Combine the chili seasoning with 1-1/2 cups of water. Add the chicken and vegetables and simmer for 15 minutes. Serve over crushed corn chips and top with cheese.

Whitemouth River

Type Mid-sized flatwater river with one section of very difficult rapids.
Difficulty Intermediate
Distance 104 km
Time 3-5 days
Access End of Hwy. #505 about 15 km south of Hadashville.
Egress Whitemouth Falls wayside park two km north of Hwy. #307 at Seven Sisters.
Topo Maps 52E12, 52E13, 62H16 and 62I1
Other Maps *Bucky's RiverRunner Guide*, Berard's Whitemouth River Routes
Season May to July

From its source, Whitemouth Lake in the Northwest Angle Provincial Forest, to the recommended access at Hwy. #505, the Whitemouth River flows for 50 kilometres through flat, marshy terrain. The river is narrow and shallow with a sand bottom. It has a surprisingly strong current and is very clear. There is one large marsh and about half a kilometre of rapids where the river flows over a rocky gravel bar. It's narrow, twisty character makes for frequent logjams and there are frequent beaver dams. Campsites are rare and small. However, it is a very pretty river and wildlife abounds, especially during spring bird migration. There are no landmarks and other signs of human activity are almost nonexistent. It is not an easy trip but the rewards in solitude and wildlife viewing are substantial. This section can be paddled at high water levels, but it requires at least two days and there are very limited camping spots.

Scenery on the Whitemouth.

Either the wayside park off Hwy. #505 or the end of Hwy. #505, where a wide turnaround leaves ample room for parking, make a good starting point for a pleasant day trip back to the Trans-Canada Highway. The river meanders for 21 kilometres past high banks covered with a mixture of spruce, fir and cedar to another wayside park off Forestry Road #30 about two kilometres south of the Trans-Canada Highway at Hadashville. After a day's paddling, a decadent delight is one of Nelda's giant cinnamon buns available at McMunn just 15 kilometres east on the highway.

There are several cottages on the west bank in the first few kilometres and, depending on water levels, some easy rapids. After about 10 kilometres the evergreen forest is left behind and an oak-aspen stand with a dense undergrowth is entered. The high banks and dense undergrowth make for few convenient stopping spots. A path on river left at 14 kilometres is an inviting spot for lunch and a stroll. At the top of the bank there is the remains of a Boy Scout camp, and several trails can be found along the river. This area appears to have been heavily logged and clear-cuts, although not visible from the river, are frequent.

Leaving the Scout camp, the river is narrower and the current correspondingly stronger as the river runs swiftly over a number of shallow gravel bars. Uprooted trees and undercut banks are often encountered in this section awaiting to upset the unwary canoeist. Hidden in the woods is a picnic shelter built for cross-country skiers using the Whitemouth River ski trails. A swinging bridge about four kilometres from the Scout camp denotes the Sandilands Forest Centre. On the right there is a self-guiding interpretive trail through a black spruce bog and deciduous and jack pine forests. A museum on the left bank has displays of local plants and logging operations. Both are worth a visit but weekdays in June are often

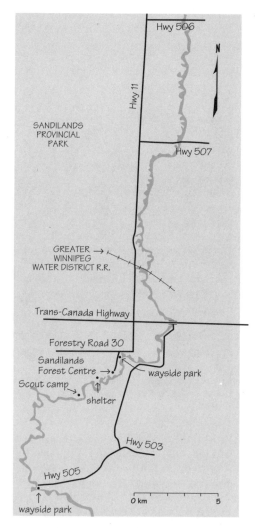

crowded with school children. Pick up a jack pine seedling from the office as a memento of your trip.

The Whitemouth River wayside park was privatized by the Manitoba government in 1991 and the present owner charges a small fee for using the boat ramp, the only take-out before the Trans-Canada Highway. After the wayside park, the sandy glacial moraine is left behind and the river meanders through a flat plain with small dairy farms along the river, never more than a few kilometres from the highway.

Reflections.

The bridge 3.2 kilometres south and east of Elma is a favourite starting place for day-trippers and adrenaline seekers wanting to play in the rapids. The river winds through flat country with generally low banks. Many farmyards and several summer homes are located on the riverbank. Aspen, oak, ash and maple line the shore, providing habitat for many varieties of birds and a screen between the river and the adjoining croplands. Whitemouth river is placid, slow moving and suitable for beginners, but the rapids are challenging and should only be attempted by intermediate canoeists. Scouting is compulsory. Often there are no portages and as the river is bordered by private land, permission should be granted before crossing a farmyard. There are many large boulders in the river, often just below the dark surface, making them difficult

to detect until you hear them scrape the bottom of your canoe. Campsites are few in number and even lunch spots are hard to find along the muddy shoreline.

The first rapid is only half a kilometre from the bridge. The portage is on river left through a farmyard. On most spring weekends canoeists can be found here playing in the rapids. All the canoeists present will offer advice or demonstrate the proper line down this class I-II rapid. It is typical of the dozen or so remaining rapids on the river; a long, fairly shallow rapid with many rocks requiring careful manoeuvring. Only Leeyus, Nevas, Ostlund and Cook's rapids have ledges that may require portaging.

Leeyus Falls is located another kilometre downstream. This is a class III ledge stretching across the river. There is a lift-over on river left. Located at the CNR mainline is a wayside park on river right and shortly thereafter the town of Elma where Hwy. #11 crosses the river. The class II rapid at the bridge is usually run on river right but in high water an exciting and usually very wet run exists on river left.

About three kilometres and two easy class I rapids past Elma, perched high on a rock overlooking the river, sits what appears to be an old orthodox church. It is actually the home of a recluse named Gary who has built it from discarded building materials. Stop for a friendly cup of tea, a tour of his fascinating home and garden, and view the many religious and other artifacts he has collected over the years. The river here charges through a narrow gap between two rocks.

You will encounter Nevas Falls shortly after leaving Gary's place, a long class I with a small island at the top, the best spot on the river for lunch. The upper section of this rapid is very wide and shallow with lots of small rocks making the deep water channel hard to find. There are two ledges separated by about 20 metres at the end of the rapid. The upper ledge, located just past the bend, is the higher of the two and cannot be seen until you have rounded the corner. Make sure you can reach the shore to avoid being accidentally swept over the ledge. It is possible to run both if a few scrapes are acceptable; the first on river left and the second on river right, but it is safer to lift-over both. The remaining rapids between Nevas and Hwy. #44 are all easy but fun to play in.

Cook's Rapids, 4.5 kilometres past Whitemouth, is the next significant rapid. It is a long class I-II with an island in the centre. Run the upper river left slowly to avoid the many rocks and take-out on shelving rock to scout the final section. This is a double drop with a massive rock to avoid at the end. There is an easy portage on the left so the final drop can be run several times.

About two kilometres past Hwy. #408, the cables of an old swinging bridge cross the river. Parishioners living on the west side used this bridge to cross the river to attend church services. Another two kilometres down river there are two massive concrete piers that supported the railway line that once spanned the river here.

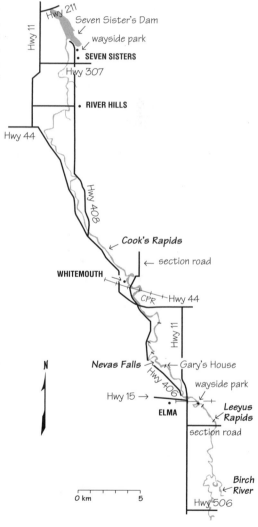

—=113=—

In 1992 a massive logjam at the class I rapid downstream from the River Hills bridge was truly impressive. At first it appeared to completely block the river, but closer examination revealed a small gap on river left leaving barely enough room to squeeze a canoe through. It is the largest logjam I have ever seen and it seems unlikely to be removed by natural causes.

The voyageurs named the river the Whitemouth because of the falls located at its mouth. This is a popular wayside park and the falls attract many anglers. While it is possible to run these falls it is not recommended as the last ledge is very shallow. There are many possible take-outs on river right so select one that minimizes portaging the canoe.

Tabouli Salad

A cool salad for a hot summer's day on the Whitemouth River.
Servings: 4
2 cups bulgur
1 tb dried onion
3 tb dried vegetables
1 peppermint tea bag
2 tb parsley flakes
1/2 cup oil
1 ts salt
1/2 ts pepper
5 tb lemon juice

Add the bulgur, onion and vegetables to 2 cups of boiling water. Steep the tea in 1/2 a cup of boiling water for 3 minutes. Discard the bag and add the tea to the bulgur. Let sit for half an hour. Add the remaining ingredients. Stir well. Let sit for half an hour.

Whiteshell River

Type A series of small, highly developed lakes connected by the Whiteshell River.
Difficulty Beginner
Distance 85 km
Time 2-3 days
Access Caddy Lake campground off Hwy. #44.
Egress Nutimik Lake campground on the Winnipeg River. There are many other egresses possible on Hwy. #307 or #309.
Topo Maps 52E14, 52L3, 52L4
Other Maps *Bucky's RiverRunner Guide*, Berard's Winnipeg River Routes, Whiteshell Provincial Park map
Season May to September

The Whiteshell River from Caddy to Betula lakes is a good first-time canoe camping trip as the government has established several designated campsites. These campsites are supplied with firepits and privies and often have picnic tables and garbage bins. The southern portion of the route is heavily used, so if you want to camp on South Cross Lake you should get there early. A cook stove is essential as open fires are not allowed and firewood is difficult to find.

From the Caddy Lake boat launch it is only a few paddle strokes to the lake where you turn left and proceed down the left side past many summer cottages. Paddle through the tunnel under the CPR railline and into South Cross Lake. This lake has several designated campsites that are in high demand. It is seven kilometres straight down the centre of the lake to the CNR mainline and the tunnel to North Cross Lake. Drift through these two low tunnels and savour the experience as the current propels you from light to darkness and back again. Be careful of motorboats coming from the opposite direction.

The first portage is at the control dam at the north end of North Cross Lake. A dam is on both sides of the island guarding the entrance to Sailing Lake and both sides are equally easy to portage.

Infamous Mouse Island is a short distance down Sailing Lake. It is the last rocky site on the lake and is a very invit-

ing campsite. However, in the past it has been infested with mice who love to invade the food packs of unsuspecting campers in the middle of the night.

From Sailing to Betula lakes the terrain is low lying and swampy with few campsites. Mallard Lake, as the name implies, is a favourite place for ducks and geese. It is a very weedy lake and difficult to paddle across in late summer or fall because of the lush vegetation clogging it. The portage at Mallard Falls is on river right and at 500 paces it is the longest on the Whiteshell River. There are several very good campsites along the portage. The rapid above the falls is a class I but inconveniently placed rocks make taking out before them difficult. The two metre-high falls are followed by a very narrow class III rapid ending in a rock garden.

Anglers are frequently seen between Mallard Lake and Whiteshell Creek. Beavers are also common along this stretch and being accustomed to boats, they can be approached quite closely. From Whiteshell Creek to Lone Island Lake the banks are muddy and covered with ash and jack pine, a pleasant change from the swamp.

At Lone Island Lake turn right and follow the right shore. A high bare rock at the north end marks the outlet of the river. Lone Island is heavily wooded down to the waterline and offers few potential campsites. There is a wayside

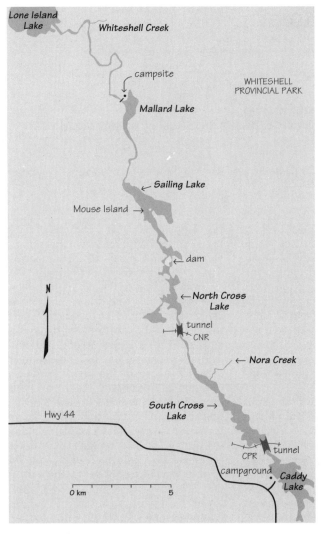

allows canoes past to the take-out at the parking lot on river right. Portage across Hwy. #307 and put-in on river right at the base of the spillway. From the highway it is half a kilometre to Rainbow Falls wayside park and White Lake. At the falls there is a lift-over on river left or an inviting slide on river right. Rainbow Falls is a very popular picnic and fishing spot and is usually crowded with vacationers during the summer.

Leaving the falls, paddle out into White Lake until you are clear of the point on the right. Once past the point, head west (right) to find a large bay to the north. Automobiles can often be seen on the highway where it skirts the northern shoreline of this bay. Follow the river for another three kilometres to the control dam and wayside park at Hwy. #307. This part of the river flows through a marsh and the shoreline is very flat with no landmarks as guides.

Another log boom guards the control dam but this one offers no easy passage for canoes. Balancing precariously on a floating log while dragging a loaded canoe across usually results in a not unexpected swim. A bathing suit is strongly recommended for this procedure.

On the north side of the road the marsh continues but the shoreline is higher. Two class I rapids between Hwy. #307 and Betula Lake prevent motorboats from coming upriver. As a result this section is not heavily travelled and wildlife sightings are more common.

park and boat launch at the north end of the lake and another one about six kilometres downstream.

After the second wayside park the river again becomes swampy, and to prolong the experience, also very winding. Jessica Lake is visible long before you arrive. At Jessica turn right and head for the radio tower to find the river outlet.

Hwy. #307 is half a kilometre downstream. There is a control dam and wayside park at the highway. A log boom spans the river to prevent swimmers from being swept over the dam. A small gap in the boom on river right

After the second rapid, paddle across a large, open marsh that continues all the way to Betula Lake. About one kilometre before Betula there is a massive rock on river right that is a good place for picnicking or camping.

At Betula Lake turn right and follow the shoreline past an island to the river exit. An open point covered with large boulders marks the river mouth. Another control dam is encountered shortly after entering the river, this one made of concrete and built in 1964. Portage 30 paces across the rock shelf in the middle of the river. From Betula to Heart Lake there are nine rapids as the river flows over frequent granite outcrops and through a mixed evergreen and aspen forest typical of the Shield. A class I- rapid after the dam leads to a 1.5 metre-high waterfall. The easiest portage is to slide your canoe down the rock face on river left, but the rock face is hidden by bush and can't be seen until the lip of the waterfall is reached—a risky task at best. There are several good campsites at this waterfall.

The next rapid is just around the corner. It is an uncanoeable rock garden at low water levels and a class II-III at higher levels. The portage should be on river right but I could find no trace of it. On the left side, the portage goes over a high rock and both the take-out and put-in are steep and narrow. A sign indicates that this rapid is called Bevbro Falls.

Located another half a kilometre downstream is Pine Point Rapids with its picnic tables, garbage cans, outhouses and hiking trails. The first two segments of this rapid are runnable. Take-out at the picnic table on river left and portage the remaining 250 paces on the hiking trail. It is tempting to line the canoes down the smooth rock face but the keeper at the end is dangerous and has caused several drownings. Pine Point is a lovely spot and can be crowded on summer weekends. Camp-

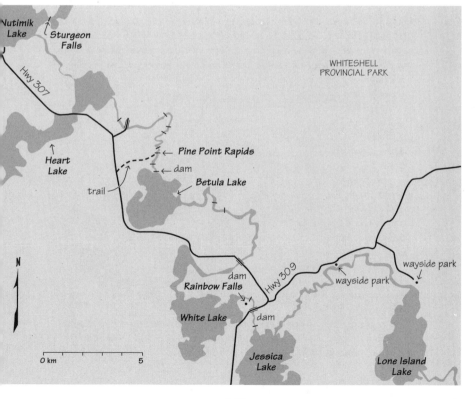

ing is not allowed. The hiking trail from Hwy. #307 continues on to Acorn and Viburnum falls. Acorn is a two metre-high waterfall with a short portage on river left. Try paddling up to the base of the falls and riding the current down.

Viburnum Falls, another kilometre downstream, is five metres high. A short portage on river left starts at the picnic table. This portage is steep and slippery when wet.

Bannock Point Rehabilitation Camp soon comes into view as well as the bridge over Caux Falls past the bend. Portage the road on river right. As there is no established trail, proceed along the shore to find a put-in. The many rocks make this rapid difficult to canoe in low water.

Two more easy runs are traversed between Caux Falls and Heart Lake. Heart Lake is another large, shallow marsh with clumps of tall grasses that make navigation difficult. Stay in the main channel and follow the map carefully to avoid getting lost. Heart Lake is a favourite nesting spot for Great Blue Herons and there are always a number of these birds soaring overhead or feeding in the shallows. Being close to the highway, they are accustomed to humans and can be approached quite closely in a canoe. The Rennie River comes in from the south and can be used as an egress by paddling a short distance upstream to Hwy. #307. The Whiteshell River continues another three kilometres to Nutimik Lake.

Past Heart Lake the river is wide and slow with waterlilies and irises lining the shore. There is a moderate amount of motorboat traffic. Nutimik Lake campground and boat launch are on the left as you leave the Whiteshell River.

Veggie Chili

When I first started canoeing my wife would freeze a large bag of chili for the first meal. Often it wouldn't be completely thawed by evening, especially on a shorter river like the Whiteshell, and the kids would complain of cold lumps in their food. This vegetarian version has no meat so it doesn't require freezing.

Servings: 4
2 cups bulgur
1 ts basil
1 ts oregano
1 can corn
1/2 ts coriander
1 bay leaf
1 dash cayenne
1 ts black pepper
1 tb cumin
1 onion and 4 cloves garlic
1 green pepper
2 tb olive oil
1 cup black bean flakes
15 oz tomatoes
6 oz tomato paste
bannock (see p. 123)

Package the dry ingredients in a plastic bag. Sauté the onion, garlic and pepper in olive oil in a pot. Add the remaining ingredients and 3 cups of water. Bring to a boil and simmer 20-30 minutes. Serve with bannock.

Winnipeg River

Type A big, high volume river with some dangerous rapids. The western section has a lot of boat traffic and is very developed.
Difficulty Intermediate
Distance 143 km
Time 4-7 days
Access Via the Whiteshell River and Crowduck Lake to Eaglenest Lake or Hwy. #313 to Pointe du Bois.
Egress Dam at Seven Sisters.
Topo Maps 52L3, 52L4, 52L5, 52L6, 62I1
Season May to September

Before the railways and highways, the Winnipeg River was the principal access to Manitoba and the vast North-West Territories. It was used by explorers, fur-traders, missionaries, the military and pioneers. The Winnipeg has been well documented from early times to the present in the writings of explorers and surveyors such as La Verendrye, Alexander Henry, David Thompson, Paul Kane, Henry Hind, George Simpson, Simon Dawson and countless others, and it would be presumptuous to repeat the material here. The construction of six hydroelectric dams and the growth of summer residences along the shore in Whiteshell Provincial Park has transformed the wild and turbulent river of fur-trade days into a chain of spacious lakes buzzing with powerboats today. At present the river is primarily of interest to canoeists interested in its history.

From the campground at Big Whiteshell Lake head east across the lake keeping to the left of the chain of islands that divides the lake. Stop at Cactus Point on the east side and inspect the prickly pear cacti growing in abundance here.

Paddle south between Post Island and the mainland. Watch for turkey vultures circling over Post Island, a favourite nesting site, and a designated campsite on the mainland. The shallow rocks in mid-channel are a favourite resting spot for cormorants and pelicans.

As you round the point and head east into Crowduck Bay, Castle Rock comes into view on your left. The view from the top is worth the climb. There is a small sand beach to land your canoe on and you can take the hard route up the front, climbing gear recommended, or stroll up the easy back route.

From Castle Rock the big yellow triangle that marks the 0.6 kilometre portage to Crowduck Lake is visible directly east. Crowduck Lake is quite clear, unlike most lakes in the Canadian Shield. It has good small mouth bass fishing in the spring and offers many fine campsites. From the portage paddle along the west shore of Crowduck, and after crossing a large bay switch to the east side and continue on to Bostrom Island. Skirt the east side of the island with its small campsite and head up a long, narrow channel to Crowduck Falls. Portage river right around the falls and try an exhilarating slide down their rock face. It is another kilometre to Eaglenest Lake, part of the immense Winnipeg River. At this point the river is a long, wide lake and requires good map reading skills to navigate the islands, points and headlands, and to stay on course.

One advantage the voyageurs never had was designated campsites. The first of these is on the east side of Levansseur Island. A small setting suitable for two to three tents, it has a sand beach, a

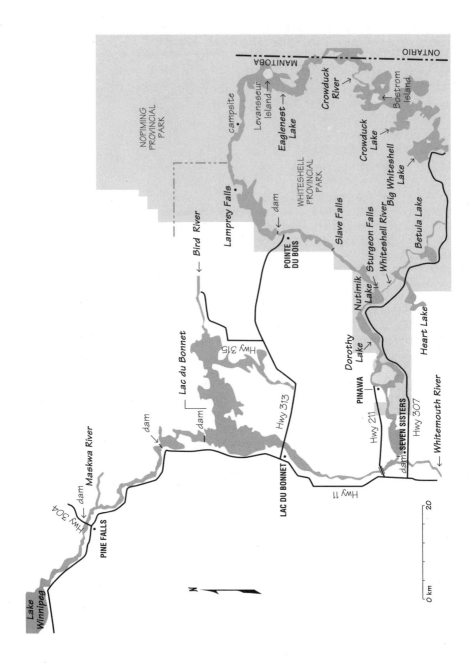

Author and Gerry Reckseidler—River Rats.

cooking shelter with firepit and stove, an outhouse and level grassy tent sites. Similar sites can be found on the island north of Greer Lake and at Lamprey Falls, another 13 kilometres and 23 kilometres downstream.

Leaving Eaglenest Lake, the river narrows some and a current is discernible, making navigation easier for the next 18 kilometres to Lamprey Falls. Depending on water levels, Lamprey can vary from fast water to a class III. However, the 10-15 foot fall described by Kane is buried deep beneath the waters. Past Lamprey Falls the river again widens to lakelike portions resulting from the dam at Pointe du Bois.

The portage at Pointe du Bois starts at a small green boathouse near the bridge and follows the road to a parking lot below the powerhouse. If the turbines are running, the portage must be extended to the end of the power channel. The portage also passes a grocery store where an ice-cream cone can be purchased. It is possible to portage left of the coffer dam, but it is very steep and requires two carries.

Two kilometres from the dam there is a campground and boat launch on river left. This can be a busy place on summer weekends with anglers fishing the Winnipeg River and nearby lakes. But it is only another eight kilometres to the more secluded Slave Falls. The portage here is on river left at the left edge of the powerhouse. The station is remotely operated and therefore deserted most of the time. It is well maintained with immaculate grounds and many well-kept buildings, a legacy of busier times. It is a very interesting place to spend several hours exploring. There is also a nice campsite on the tiny island two kilometres downstream.

Situated 10 kilometres below Slave Falls is Sturgeon Falls, the only rapid left on the once tumultuous Winnipeg. Like Lamprey, Sturgeon can range from a class I to a monstrous class III+ depending on water levels. It is difficult to imagine the ferocity of this rapid before it was drowned by the Seven Sisters Dam in 1931.

Cottage country on the Winnipeg extends from Sturgeon Falls to Pinawa. Several campgrounds and even a restaurant or two can be found along this stretch of river. If you plan your trip properly you can eat all your meals in restaurants and not have to carry food.

After Pinawa the land is much flatter and the shoreline is mostly willow and cattails. Natalie Lake has a very low shoreline, making it hard to tell where lake ends and land starts. A rock retaining dam almost completely surrounds the lake.

At Seven Sisters portage to the right of the powerhouse at the start of the rock dam. Follow the road through the parking lot to the put-in at the base of the powerhouse and paddle out tailrace. On the left side of the powerhouse there is a visitor's gallery where you can view the turbines and if fortunate, get a tour.

Leaving the tailrace of Seven Sisters, the Whitemouth River on the left and Hwy. #211 bridge on the right are both visible. Both locations have picnic sites. From here to Lac du Bonnet the land on both sides of the river is private. Located on river right is the Whiteshell nuclear research station where landing is prohibited.

Past the town of Lac du Bonnet the river widens into the largest lake encountered yet, and three more hydro dams have to be portaged before reaching Lake Winnipeg. The shoreline is mostly private and the public land is often low, swampy and unsuitable for camping. There are two small picnic sites located beside Hwy. #11. The Fort Alexander Indian Reserve occupies both sides of the river between Pine Falls and Lake Winnipeg.

If you are continuing past Pine Falls it will be necessary to paddle Traverse Bay to take-out at the community of Victoria Beach or Traverse Bay. Lake Winnipeg is regarded by many as more dangerous than even Lake Superior as the wind can raise huge waves in this shallow lake very quickly. Therefore continuing south to the Red River is not recommended.

Jeannine's Bannock

Bannock is the traditional bread of the fur trade. It was introduced by the Hudson's Bay Co. and quickly adapted by travellers in the west because of its light weight and quick cooking. Spice up the plain bannock with fresh berries, grated cheese, raisins, fish or the traditional buffalo meat and prepare it on the Winnipeg River, the principal river of the fur trade.

Servings: This recipe makes 7 bannocks and each bannock will serve 4 people.

20 cups flour
1 lb lard
1 cup powdered milk
1 cup baking powder
1 cup sugar
1/4 cup salt

At home, cut the lard into the flour. Add the remaining ingredients, mix well and package in leakproof containers. A mixture of half whole wheat and half white flour works well. To vary the taste add a handful of any of the following: raisins, dried cranberries, cheese, gorp or fresh berries such as blueberries or saskatoons. Make a well in the centre, pour in 1/4 cup of water and mix quickly. The dough should be stiff and evenly moist. Form the dough into a round ball, then flatten the ball into a 10 inch greased or non-stick fry pan and bake on low fire about 15 minutes per side. Or use an Outback Oven—it makes an excellent bannock.

Useful Information

Tourism and Paddling

Manitoba Natural Resources
Parks Branch
200 Saulteaux Cres.
Winnipeg, MB
R3J 3W3
(204) 945-6784

Manitoba Naturalists Society
401 - 63 Albert St.
Winnipeg, MB
R3B 1G4
(204) 943-9029

Manitoba Recreational Canoeing Association
P.O. Box 2663
Winnipeg, MB
R3C 4B3
(204) 925-5681
http://kohlrabi.cs.umanitoba.ca/mrca/mrca.html

Wave Track Canoes
42C Speers Road
Winnipeg, MB
R2J 1M3
(204) 231-8226
fax: (204) 231-8227
gbrabant@infobahn.mb.ca
http://www.wilds.mb.ca/paddle/wavetrack

Wilderness Supply Co.
623 Ferry Road
Winnipeg, MB
R3H 0T5
phone & fax: (204) 783-9555

Maps

Global Village Map and Travel Store
167 Lilac St.
Winnipeg, MB
R3M 2S1
(204) 475-3254
fax: (204) 475-3256
glovillg@pangea.ca

Manitoba Natural Resources
Surveys and Mapping Branch
1007 Century Ave.
Winnipeg, MB
R3H 0W4
(204) 945-6666
fax: (204) 945-1365
mapsales@nr.gov.mb.ca

Travel Manitoba
21 Forks Market Road
Winnipeg, MB
R3C 4T7
(204) 945-3777
(800) 665-0040
fax: (204) 948-2517
http://www.gov.mb.ca/Travel-Manitoba

Outfitters

Aksarnerk Adventures
230 Barker Blvd.
Winnipeg, MB
R3R 2E4
(204) 895-0001

Batstone Canoe Pickup
Box 531
Churchill, MB
R0B 0E0
(204) 675-2300

Big Rock Hunting Fishing Lodge
Box 170
Gypsumville, MB
R0C 1J0
mobile JR4 2807

Bissett Outfitters
Lot 46, Antonio Road
Bissett, MB
R0E 0J0
(204) 277-5262
fax: (204) 277-5538

Bloodvein River Outfitters
Box 1083
Lac du Bonnet, MB
R0E 1A0
(204) 345-8002

Child's Lake Lodge
Box 13
Boggy Creek, MB
R0L 0G0
(204) 546-2746

Clearwater Canoe Outfitters
Box 3939
The Pas, MB
R9A 1K7
(204) 624-5606

Delta Marsh Canoe Trips
Box 23
St. Ambroise, MB
R0H 1G0
(204) 243-2009

Dymond Lake Outfitters
Box 304
Churchill, MB
R0B 0E0
(204) 675-8875

Einarsson's Guide Service
Box 149
Gypsumville, MB
R0C 1J0
(204) 659-4573

Grass River Outfitters
Box 59
Wabowden, MB
R0B 1S0
(204) 689-2022

Great Canadian Ecoventures
Box 25181-T
Winnipeg, MB
R2V 4C8
(800) 667-WILD
fax (604) 733-8657

Northern Manitoba Outfitters
General Delivery
Berens River, MB
R0B 0A0
(204) 382-2379

North River Outfitters
80 Deerwood Dr.
Thompson, MB
R8N 1E1
(204) 778-6979

Nu-Cho Expeditions
83 Char Bay
Thompson, MB
R8N 1P4
(204) 677-9158

Parkland Outfitters
Box 87
Inglis, MB
R0J 0X0
(204) 564-2201

Raven Eye Outfitters
P.O. Box 698
Lynn Lake, MB
R0B 0W0
(204) 356-2243
(888) 463-6736
http://www.wilds.mb.ca/paddle/raveneye/

Souris River Adventures
Box 688
Deloraine, MB
R0M 0M0
(204) 747-2683

Spence's Mantario Outfitters
General Delivery
Bissett, MB
R0E 0J0
(204) 277-5232

Tan Lake Outfitters
Box 123
Gypsumville, MB
R0C 1J0
(204) 659-5284

Waterhen Band Outfitting
General Delivery
Skownan, MB
R0L 1Y0
(204) 628-3320

Wekusko Falls Canoeing
Box 705
Snow Lake, MB
R0B 1M0
(204) 358-2270

Wellman Lake Lodge
Box 249
Minitona, MB
R0L 1G0
(204) 525-4452

Wilderness Adventures, YM-YWCA
100 - 290 Vaughan St.
Winnipeg, MB
R3B 2N8
(204) 942-8157

Wilderness Odysseys Ltd.
Box 30355
Alexandria, VA 22310
USA
(412) 329-0436
(800) 443-6199

Wild-Wise Inc.
825 Sherbrook St.
Winnipeg, MB
R3A 1M5
(204) 783-9828
fax: (204) 786-0860

Wolf Lake Wilderness
Box 383
Selkirk, MB
R1A 2B3
(204) 788-4170

WoodMac Outdoor Equipment
414 Main St. N.
Dauphin, MB
R7N 1C8
(204) 638-6149

Charters and Transport

Bissett Air Service
Lot 46, Antonio Road
Bissett, MB
R0E 0J0
(204) 277-5262
fax: (204) 277-5538

Keewatin Air
1-1692 Dublin Ave.
Winnipeg, MB
R3H 1A8
(204) 632-6621
fax: (204) 632-8777

LaRonge Aviation
Box 940
Lynn Lake, MB
R0B 0W0
(204) 356-2457
fax: (204) 356-8018

Northway Aviation
Box 70
Arnes, MB
R0C 0C0
(204) 642-5631
fax: (204) 642-8160

Northwinds Air
204 - 83 Churchill Dr.
Thompson, MB
R8N 0L6
(204) 677-7850

RnD Aviation
Box 609, Leaf Rapids, MB
R0B 1W0
(204) 473-2963
fax: (204) 473-8123

Selkirk Air Services
Box 2, Grp. 214, RR2
Selkirk, MB
R1A 2A7
(204) 482-3270

Skyward Aviation
P.O. Box 1027
Thompson, MB
R8N 1P1
(204) 778-7088

Wamair Service
General Delivery
Matheson Island, MB
R0C 2A0
(204) 276-2410

Waterways Enterprises
548 Dunrobin St.
Winnipeg, MB
R2K 0V2
(204) 668-8339

Whiteshell Air Service
Box 975
Lac du Bonnet, MB
R0E 1A0
(204) 345-8339

Kilometrage Chart

Distances from Winnipeg to suggested river access and egress

Bernic Lake Rd. @ Hwy. #315	148 km
Bernic Lake Rd. @ Bird River	154 km
Birch Falls Wayside Park	240 km
Bird River (Hwy. #315)	137 km
Bird River (Tulabi Falls)	174 km
Bissett, MB	230 km
Black Lake Campground	191 km
Black River (Hwy. #304)	150 km
Black River (Hwy. #314)	186 km
Caribou Landing	238 km
Currie's Landing Wayside Park	219 km
Elma, MB	77 km
Gardenton, MB (Hwy. #209)	103 km
Gem Lake Road	170 km
Grand Valley (Assiniboine River)	209 km
Lac du Bonnet, MB	97 km
Lee River (Hwy. #313)	141 km
Manigotagan River (Hwy. #304)	180 km
Matheson Landing	216 km
Moose River (Hwy. #314)	206 km
Nutimik Lake Campground	125 km
Ochre River @ Skane Crossing	275 km
Pembina River @ Hwy. #31	135 km
Pinawa, MB	107 km
Pine Falls, MB	108 km
Rabbit River (Hwy. #314)	184 km
Rennie River (Hwy. #307)	127 km
Rivers, MB	234 km
Riverton, MB	115 km
Roseau River, MB	79 km
Roseau River @ U.S. border	132 km
Senkiw Ford	73 km
Stuartburn (Hwy. #201)	86 km
Valley River (Hwy. #274)	336 km
Valley River (Hwy. #362)	320 km
Wallace Lake via Hwy. #304 (Pine Falls)	251 km
Wallace Lake via Hwy. #314 (Lac Du Bonnet)	210 km
Wanipigow Campground	204 km
Whitemouth River (Hwy. #307)	89 km
Whitemouth River (Hwy. #505)	100 km
Whitemouth River Falls	91 km
Whiteshell River (Hwy. #307)	141 km

Available from Rocky Mountain Books

Planning a Wilderness Trip in Canada & Alaska, Keith Morton, 384p., $29.95
Essential reading for anyone planning a wilderness trip in North America.

GPS Made Easy, Lawrence Letham, 112p., $14.95
Includes practical examples using handheld GPS receivers in the outdoors.

Canoeing Safety and Rescue, Doug McKown, 128p., $12.95
Essential reading for recreational canoe paddlers who need to be self sufficient.

Nahanni: the River Guide, Peter Jowett, 224p., $15.95
A comprehensive guide to the South Nahanni and Flat rivers.

Summits and Icefields, Chic Scott, 304p., $15.95
Alpine ski tours in the Rockies and Columbia mountains of western Canada.

Ski Trails in the Canadian Rockies, Chic Scott, 224p., $14.95
Cross-country ski trails: groomed, backcountry and easy tours above treeline.

Waterfall Ice Climbs in the Canadian Rockies, Joe Josephson, 272p., $19.95
A wide selection of ice climbs on both sides of the Canadian Rockies.

Selected Alpine Climbs in the Canadian Rockies, Sean Dougherty, 320p., $19.95
An up-to-date guide to the best mountaineering routes in the Canadian Rockies.

Scrambles in the Canadian Rockies, Alan Kane, 208p., $14.95
A guide to 102 non-technical peaks for mountain scramblers.

Kananaskis Country Trail Guide, Gillean Daffern, 2 vols., 272p., $15.95 each
The third edition of this popular guide to Alberta's Kananaskis Country.

Kananaskis Country Ski Trails, Gillean Daffern, 296p., $14.95
Ski opportunities from groomed trails to ski touring routes and telemark hills.

Backcountry Biking in the Canadian Rockies, Eastcott & Lepp, 352p., $16.95
Over 200 trails and old roads in the Rocky Mountains of Alberta and B.C.

To order write or fax to:
Rocky Mountain Books, #4 Spruce Centre SW
Calgary, Alberta T3C 3B3, Canada
Fax: 403-249-2968, Tel: 403-249-9490
If you live in western USA or Canada phone **1-800-566-3336**
We accept cheques or Visa (sorry we do not accept other credit cards)
Visit our web site at: http://www.culturenet.ca/rmb/